Three Dimensions of Vocabulary Growth

Lewis M. Paternoster

Associate Professor of English
Housatonic Community College
Bridgeport, Connecticut

Ruth L. Frager

Professor of English
Chairman of the English Department
Housatonic Community College
Bridgeport, Connecticut

Three Dimensions of Vocabulary Growth

When ordering this book, please specify:
either **R 106 P** *or* THREE DIMENSIONS OF VOCABULARY GROWTH

AMSCO SCHOOL PUBLICATIONS, INC.

315 Hudson Street New York, N.Y. 10013

ISBN 0-87720-345-8

Printed in the United States of America

Preface

This book presents three methods for learning new words. The basic technique of all three methods is to learn some additional fact about a word when learning the word and its definition.

The First Dimension. A word may have an interesting history behind it. Words with stories behind them remain fresh and vivid in the memory, and become a permanent part of one's working vocabulary. Part I, The Romance of Words, presents the histories of many such words.

The Second Dimension. A word may have a particularly striking etymology. Etymologies are especially valuable as mnemonic devices because they are often evoked by the word itself. In effect, the word defines itself through the word elements of which it is composed. Words with graphic and memorable etymologies are treated in Part II, Etymologies.

The Third Dimension. Many words fall naturally into categories or groups of words with related meanings. When a new word is learned, it can be placed in such a category and distinguished from other words related to the same general idea. The new word then becomes a ready and precise vocabulary tool that can be used with effectiveness and confidence. This simple but effective mnemonic technique is presented in Part III, Related Words.

Another mnemonic device used throughout the book is repetition. Many words appear in more than one exercise. A few words appear as main entries in more than one lesson. And words appearing as main entries frequently reappear in the body of the text.

The exercises following each lesson have two aims. One aim is to test and reinforce students' knowledge of the words they have studied. The other is to strengthen their understanding of the method under consideration. In accordance with the latter objective, many of the exercises in Part I and II focus on etymons and word elements as such. The authors believe that familiarity with etymons and word elements is not only an effective means of remembering words, but also a way of making words more meaningful.

Exercises are of a wide variety of types, including matching tests, multiple-choice, word-completion and sentence-completion, true-false, dictionary research, and definition of words and word elements.

Students and instructors should understand that this is not a vocabulary book in the usual sense. The typical vocabulary book seeks to teach students words, or perhaps to teach them something *about* words. The primary function of this book, on the other hand, is to impart the habit of learning *from* words. Words are more eloquent than anything that could be said about them. To understand that fact is to be well on the way to vocabulary growth.

L.M.P.
R.L.F.

Contents

The First Dimension: **The Romance of Words**

The Second Dimension: **Etymologies**

Key to Abbreviations

adj. adjective
adv. adverb
n. noun
v.i. intransitive verb
v.t. transitive verb

The First Dimension

The Romance of Words

How did people who could not read or write remember facts? One way was to tell stories about them. There is no doubt that a fact stays in the memory longer if it is associated with other facts or fits into a larger pattern. The same holds true for words. If you know an interesting story behind a word, you are likely to remember that word.

This first part of your word study shows how you can remember some words by learning their interesting histories. Each word is followed by a brief account of its origin, its current meaning, and, where necessary, an explanation of how the word acquired its present meaning. The catch word or phrase immediately following each word is not a definition, but rather a handy reminder of the story that goes with the word.

Following each lesson are three exercises. The first, a multiple-choice exercise, tests your knowledge of the words occurring in the same lesson as the exercise. The second, a matching exercise, tests your mastery of the words in the lesson immediately preceding. The matching exercises begin with Lesson 2. The third exercise offers a selection of new words to look up in the dictionary. By re-creating the histories behind these words, you will make them a part of your permanent vocabulary.

LESSON 1

nefarious not right (*adj.*)

The Latin *nefarius*, derived from *nefas*, meaning "crime" or "wrong," gives us the word *nefarious*. *Nefas*, a compound of *ne* (not) + *fas* (lawful), lacks the strong sense of its English derivative *nefarious*, which means "flagrantly wicked, evil, villainous." Nevertheless, *nefarious* retains the root sense of "not right," particularly since the word implies conscious intent to do wrong.

palpable stroke, caress (*adj.*)

From the Latin *palpare*, "to stroke or caress," which implies the presence of an object that can be touched, we derive our word *palpable*: "able to be touched or perceived, tangible." We apply the word not only to objects that can be seen, felt, smelled, or tasted, but also to acts, ideas, or impressions that are clear to the mind or intellect.

picayune coin (*adj.*)

This word comes from the French *picaillon*, an old copper coin. In the United States, certain small coins similar to five-cent pieces were known as picayunes. *Picayune* now means "of relatively little value or worth." Compare this to the meaning of *trivial*.

plagiarize kidnaper (*v.t., v.i.*)

The word *plagiarize* is of Latin origin. It is built on the Latin word *plagiarius*, which means "kidnaper." A *plagiarist* is one who steals or appropriates the work (a play, a novel, or an idea) of another person and passes it off as his own. A writer who does not intend to publish his writing may legitimately use the work of another author as long as he gives full credit to the original author (as in a footnote). If the writer fails to give proper credit, however, he is a plagiarist.

prestidigitation nimble fingers (*n.*)

This long word certainly presents a formidable appearance. Its derivation, however, is quite simple. *Preste* (nimble) + *digitus* (finger) form the word. A *prestidigitator* is a sleight-of-hand artist, or magician. A capable prestidigitator can make objects appear or disappear as though he possessed some occult power. Actually, all he needs is a pair of quick hands, or "nimble fingers."

sarcophagus eating flesh (*n.*)

The Greek *sarkophagos* means, literally, "eating flesh." The material used in the construction of coffins was a limestone which is highly corrosive. Within a period of several weeks, the limestone would disintegrate the cadaver within the coffin. A *sarcophagus* is a large coffin usually, though not necessarily, found in a tomb.

scapegoat escaped goat (*n.*)

The concept of the word *scapegoat* has a long history, dating back to the early Jews. The original scapegoat was an actual goat upon whose head were symbolically placed all the sins of the tribe or community. The animal was allowed to "escape" into the wilderness, carrying the tremendous burden of sin with it and thus relieving the people (see Leviticus 16:8–22 in the Old Testament). Today the word *scapegoat* has a similar connotation. A scapegoat is one who has become the butt of another's misdeeds or to whom some form of blame or guilt is transferred.

sycophant accuser (*n.*)

This word is built on two Greek elements: *sykos* (a fig) + *phainein* (to show). Some persons attempting to curry favor with those in high places became informers, advancing themselves by offering to denounce criminals to the authorities. A criminal was pointed out by a sign known as the "gesture of the fig." Consequently, one who made this gesture became an accuser. The word *sycophant* denotes a person who is willing to demean himself by being a "yes-man" or an "apple polisher" for selfish, personal reasons.

syndrome run together (*n.*)

A *syndrome* is a cluster of symptoms occurring together and indicating that a patient has a particular disease. The Greek *syn*, as you may know, means "together." You will recognize the Greek source word *dramein* (to run) in such other English words as *dromedary* (literally, "runner") and *hippodrome* ("racetrack"—from *hippos*, "horse"). The word *syndrome* has become part of psychiatric vocabulary; for example, "He has a paranoia syndrome." Often it denotes a pathological condition. We have weakened the word somewhat by applying it to almost any group or movement that we feel has "symptoms"; for example, the *youth syndrome* of American women, or the *flower syndrome* of the hippy generation.

trivial three ways (*adj.*)

The word *trivial* comes from the Latin *tri* (three) + *via* (way) and means, literally, "like something found at a place where three roads meet." If you glance at a map of Italy, you will see many places where three roads meet. In ancient times, as now, such places must have been frequented by many travelers, and events there would seldom be out of the ordinary. Hence our definition of *trivial:* "found everywhere, common, insignificant." Can you determine the meaning of *trivia*? Check your answer against the dictionary definition.

EXERCISES

A. Select the word or phrase that best completes the sentence.

1. A *plagiarist* is a person who (*a*) writes plays (*b*) holds another person for ransom (*c*) uses footnotes (*d*) pretends that another person's writings or ideas are his own (*e*) satirizes another author.
2. A *scapegoat* is (*a*) another name for the Book of Leviticus (*b*) a tormentor (*c*) one who bears the blame for others

(*d*) a clay figurine of a goat worshipped by primitive people (*e*) a burnt offering.

3. A *trivial* occurrence is one (*a*) having three distinct results (*b*) having little importance (*c*) happening in three places at once (*d*) happening at the crossroads (*e*) of special significance.
4. A *sarcophagus* is (*a*) a flesh-eating animal (*b*) a corpse (*c*) a large coffin (*d*) a sharp cough (*e*) a monument.
5. *Picayune* now means (*a*) of little value (*b*) complex (*c*) a small-sized coin (*d*) distasteful (*e*) a little one.
6. A *prestidigitator* is (*a*) a political agitator (*b*) a man of prestige (*c*) a pickpocket (*d*) an imposter (*e*) a sleight-of-hand artist.
7. A *nefarious* deed indicates an act that is (*a*) legal (*b*) wicked (*c*) secret (*d*) intentional (*e*) generous.
8. *Palpable* implies something (*a*) tangible (*b*) credible (*c*) pale (*d*) pulsating (*e*) objectionable.
9. A *sycophant* would be an expert in the art of (*a*) fig growing (*b*) flattery (*c*) psychoanalysis (*d*) stealing (*e*) fishing.
10. A *syndrome* is a group of (*a*) businessmen (*b*) airplanes (*c*) symptoms (*d*) bees (*e*) newspapers.

B. Using a collegiate dictionary or an unabridged dictionary, look up the etymology and the definition of each of the following words. Then write a brief explanation of how you think each word developed its modern meaning.

1. absolve
2. adamant
3. alchemy
4. alderman
5. allegory
6. ally
7. amen
8. apocalyptic
9. curriculum
10. glamor

LESSON 2

bombast cotton (*n.*)

Most of us have heard speakers use highly artificial and inflated language. Such language is termed *bombast* and is described as *bombastic*. The word *bombast* comes from the Old French *bombace*, meaning "cotton" or "stuff used for padding." Hence our word *bombast*, which suggests extravagant, artificial language padded with words.

catholic universal; general (*adj.*)

Derived from the Greek *katholikos*, combined of *kata* (completely) + *holos* (whole), the word *catholic* spelled with a lower case "c" is today often a puzzle to those who are acquainted with its meaning only when spelled with a capital "C." *Roman Catholic* refers to a particular church that subscribes to a specific creed, ritual, and belief. *Greek Catholic* denotes another specific church. When Protestants recite the Apostles' Creed, however, they say, "I believe in the holy catholic church," meaning that they believe in a universal church of which Christ is the spiritual head.

The Ecumenical Council promoting union of Christian churches often calls attention to the word *catholic* as a common denominator unifying various divisions of the Christian faith. The word may also be used to refer to any universality; for example, "His tastes in reading are catholic" or "The catholicity of his belief in man qualifies him for the presidency of the Ecumenical Council."

delirium to go out of the furrow in plowing (*n.*)

The definition of our word *delirium* is not as implausible as its etymology may indicate. The Latin *de-* (out) + *lira* (furrow) combined to form a word designating the wandering of a plow from the straight line set for a furrow. In other words, either the farmer directing the plow or the animal pulling the plow deviated from a straight line. *Delirium* denotes mental wandering, confusion, disorganized speech, or frenzied emotional excitement. The word is thus linked to its origin, for it signifies behavior that deviates from a line we think of as normal or straight.

ecumenical the inhabited world (*adj.*)

From the Greek *oikumenē*, meaning "the inhabited world" or "the whole world," we derive our word *ecumenical*, meaning "worldwide in extent." Today the word is used most widely in reference to the movement promoting universal Christianity and cooperation, particularly the merging of Protestant sects with each other and the larger merging of Roman Catholicism and Protestantism. Sometimes still spelled "*oecumenical*," the word may be used correctly in referring to any type of worldwide unity as well as the specific unity of the whole of a body of churches.

laconic Laconia (region in the southwestern peninsula of Greece whose capital was Sparta) (*adj.*)

The word *laconic* means "using language sparingly," or getting directly to the point. The inhabitants of ancient Laconia were very reticent. It was reported that during a siege of Sparta, the Laconian capital, a Roman general sent a note to the Laconian commander stating that if he captured the city he would burn it to the ground. The laconic reply from within the city gates read, "If!" Another story that may serve as a mnemonic aid in strengthening your retention of the word deals with President Calvin Coolidge, said to have been one of our most laconic statesmen. One evening at a dinner given in his honor, President Coolidge was approached by a comely young female reporter who with a winsome smile said to the President, "Mr. President, I bet my fellow reporters twenty-five dollars that I could get you to say more than two words." Coolidge replied laconically, "You lose."

maudlin Magdalene (*adj.*)

The Gospel of St. Luke contains a story of a repentant sinner who showed her love for Jesus by washing his feet with her tears. The weeping woman, traditionally identified with Mary Magdalene, became a favorite subject of medieval and Renaissance painting.

The tearful Mary was portrayed so sentimentally that eventually her name became synonymous with "tearfully sentimental." The English word *maudlin* reflects the pronunciation of the Old French *Maudelene. Maudlin* means "tearfully sentimental" or "crying at the slightest provocation." The word is often applied to those who become easily tearful when they have drunk more alcohol than they have a capacity for.

ostracize shell; potsherd (*v.t.*)

Ostrakon is a Greek word meaning "shell" or "potsherd." From this we get the English word *ostracize*, meaning "to ban," or "to exclude from a group by popular consent." In ancient Athens a citizen could be banished by popular vote of other citizens. The voting was done by dropping pottery fragments, or potsherds, into an urn. Each potsherd bore the name of a person the voter wished to have banished. The person whose name appeared on the greatest number of potsherds was sent away from the city, or ostracized.

sincere without wax (*adj.*)

Surely we all know the meaning of the word *sincere*. We may not know, however, an interesting and romantic history traditionally assigned to it. During an era in Rome when pottery-making was at its peak, the word was coined to meet a specific need of the time. Pottery-making was and still is a delicate craft. No matter how careful the artisan is during firing or drying of the clay, accidents often occur which result in cracks or other damage to the finished product. When this happened to the Roman pottery-maker, he could either discard the defective piece or attempt repair. If he decided to repair, he would cover the imperfection by filling it with wax and painting over the patch. He could then sell the piece without taking too much chance of being apprehended in his deceit. The word *sincere*, so the story goes, originally meant "without wax" (*sin*, "without" + *cera*, "wax"), signifying that a piece of pottery was without cracks or defects that had been covered up with wax. Hence we get our word *sincere*, meaning "true; without deceit; honest; unadulterated."

spurious of illegitimate birth; bastard (*adj.*)

The Latin *spurius*, meaning "false," provides the etymology for the English *spurious*, meaning "counterfeit." We speak of a spurious painting or a spurious ten-dollar bill.

EXERCISES

A. Select the word or phrase that best completes the sentence.

1. *Delirium* implies (*a*) contagious diseases (*b*) strenuous effort (*c*) delight (*d*) temporary mental confusion (*e*) laziness.
2. People who become *maudlin* over the problems of fictional characters are (*a*) unnecessarily critical (*b*) sentimentally tearful (*c*) snobbish (*d*) compassionately understanding (*e*) sadistic.
3. A *bombastic* speech is (*a*) persuasively logical (*b*) unnecessarily loud (*c*) unnecessarily extravagant (*d*) excessively severe (*e*) poorly organized.
4. To *ostracize* a person is to (*a*) honor him (*b*) ridicule him (*c*) banish him (*d*) injure him (*e*) imitate him.
5. A *catholic* point of view is (*a*) religious (*b*) dictated by the Pope (*c*) universal in scope (*d*) restricted by business interests (*e*) dependent upon formal education.
6. A *sincere* offer is one that is (*a*) attractive (*b*) implicit (*c*) honest (*d*) shrewd (*e*) final.
7. A *spurious* dollar bill is (*a*) torn (*b*) counterfeit (*c*) splotched (*d*) first issue (*e*) spurned.
8. An *ecumenical* meeting is one that is (*a*) attended by dignitaries (*b*) called for the purpose of electing political candidates (*c*) held every ten years (*d*) conducted in a cathedral (*e*) worldwide in scope.
9. A *laconic* person (*a*) is stingy (*b*) is Spartan (*c*) likes milk (*d*) uses few words (*e*) is tense.

B. Match each word in column A with its definition in column B.

Column A	*Column B*
1. sycophant	*a.* to steal ideas
2. plagiarize	*b.* one who bears the blame for others
3. scapegoat	*c.* sleight-of-hand artist
4. picayune	*d.* flatterer
5. prestidigitator	*e.* evil
6. sarcophagus	*f.* group of symptoms
7. nefarious	*g.* of little worth
8. palpable	*h.* stone coffin
9. syndrome	*i.* tangible; obvious

C. Using a collegiate dictionary or an unabridged dictionary, look up the etymology and the definition of each of the following words. Then write a brief explanation of how you think each word developed its modern meaning.

1. arbor
2. babble
3. calisthenics
4. caterpillar
5. chagrin
6. charlatan
7. chimera
8. condescend

LESSON 3

akimbo jug handle (*adj.*, *adv.*)

The expression *arms akimbo* is used quite frequently to describe a position in which a person's hands are placed on the hips with the elbows extended outward. The expression comes from the Middle English word *kenebowe*, which means "jug handle." The picture of someone standing arms akimbo—looking like a two-handled jug—is strikingly vivid.

blatant bleat (*adj.*)

The word *blatant* is actually a variant form of the word *bleat.* Have you ever heard a flock of sheep bleat? If you have, you will know the meaning of *blatant*—"noisy; clamorous." We use the word in connection with things seen as well as heard to mean too conspicuous or showy.

egregious apart from the herd (*adj.*)

This word, coming from the Latin *e* (out) + *grex* or *gregis* (herd), expresses the opposite of the idea of selection for excellence or eminence. That which is *egregious* is "set apart from the herd" on the basis of *undesirable* qualities. *Egregious*, then, means "remarkably bad."

gauche left (*adj.*)

The English word *gauche* means "clumsy or awkward, especially in social situations." We use the word to indicate a lack of tact, such as asking the boss's wife how much she paid for the dress she is wearing. It can also be used in a more general sense to indicate any kind of social awkwardness or clumsiness. The development of *gauche* into its modern English meaning is rather obscure. It may have originated in the Middle French word *gauchir*, meaning "to turn aside" or "to detour," which later took on the meaning of "bent" or "askew," finally arriving (still in French) at the meaning "left." If we consider the logical extension of the word "right" from the direction "right" to the idea of "proper" or "correct," it is not difficult to reason in the same way from the direction "left" to the idea of (socially) "improper," "incorrect," or "clumsy."

gratuitous grateful (*adj.*)

From the Latin *gratia* (favor; thanks) and the form *gratus* (grateful), we derive our word *gratuitous*, meaning "free; without charge." The word *gratuitous* is also used, especially by the school of existential philosophy, to denote an action done without cause or justification. A gratuitous crime, for instance, might be a murder done with absolutely no cause to a person completely unknown to the murderer.

peer equal (*n.*)

The word *peer* is built on the Latin *par*, meaning "equal"; hence a group of your peers is a group of people on a par with you in some areas. For instance, if you were to be compared with other students in relation to your grades, you might be compared to a *peer group*—a group equal to you in native intelligence, potential, and ability. Social or economic situation, job status, or cultural background may also serve as factors in deciding who is your peer. Why then do we use the expression, "The accused will be judged by a jury of his peers"?

sinister on the left (*adj.*)

The word *sinister* suggests either an evil force or an evil motivation. The Latin word *sinister*, meaning "on the left," implied something evil because in augury the left side was regarded as unlucky. The word *sinister* today has taken on the coloration of wickedness because of this early association with prophecies of bad luck.

travesty to disguise (*n.*)

Travesty, derived from the Latin *trans* (over; across) + *vestire* (to dress; attire), means "a ludicrous distortion." The word originally referred to people who dressed up in grotesque clothing in order to ridicule. We apply the word less literally today; for example, to make a travesty of justice is to disguise a flagrant miscarriage of justice, thus making a mockery of it.

venal sale (*adj.*)

A *venal* sin or crime is outstandingly bad, for the malefactor has in effect sold principle, honor, and integrity. Derived from the Latin *venalis*, "capable of being bought," the word *venal* has acquired the sense of "able to be bought off; mercenary; corrupt." Probably the most famous examples of sinners who committed venal sins are Judas, in his betrayal of Christ, and Faust, who sold his soul to the Devil. These figures and others who have been corrupted by money have become subjects of much great literature and art.

venial pardon (*adj.*)

The word *venial* is often confused with the word *venal*. The difference between the two is great. *Venial* is derived from the Latin word *venia*, meaning "pardon." A *venial* sin, therefore, is one that is pardonable; a *venal* sin, whether pardonable or not, is one that is committed for money. Keep these distinctions in mind, for to accuse a man of a *venal* sin when you intend *venial* is similar to accusing of assault and battery a man who bruises someone by accident.

vixen she-fox (*n.*)

The Anglo-Saxon word for *vixen* is *fyxen*, the feminine form of the Old English word *fox*. Our word *vixen* means "a shrewish, ill-tempered woman." English has many uncomplimentary terms for women; for instance, *shrew*, a word made famous by a Shakespeare play; *shrike*, used as the title of a play popular in the 1950's; *fishwife*; *harridan*. Can you think of similarly uncomplimentary terms for men in our language? Or does English have a built-in bias against women?

EXERCISES

A. Select the word or phrase that best completes the sentence.

1. A *sinister* person (*a*) is left-handed (*b*) appears to be evil (*c*) appears to be clumsy (*d*) has good intentions (*e*) holds strong opinions.
2. To stand with arms *akimbo* means to stand (*a*) with hands on hips and elbows out (*b*) with arms crossed over the chest (*c*) with arms outstretched and elbows bent (*d*) with arms hanging loose (*e*) with hands behind the back.
3. A *vixen* is (*a*) an animal known also as a shrew (*b*) a synonym for "woman" (*c*) a bird of prey (*d*) a vampire (*e*) an ill-tempered woman.
4. To be *gauche* is to be (*a*) nauseated (*b*) awkward (*c*) evil (*d*) right-handed (*e*) exhausted.
5. A *gratuitous* action is one rendered (*a*) freely (*b*) in anticipation of receiving a tip (*c*) under duress (*d*) for selfish reasons (*e*) out of gratitude.
6. A *blatant* objection is one that is (*a*) anticipated (*b*) noisy (*c*) bland (*d*) sincere (*e*) unnecessary.
7. An *egregious* failure is (*a*) a remarkably bad failure (*b*) a slight mistake (*c*) a doubtful failure (*d*) a tragic failure (*e*) a public failure.
8. A judgment by one's *peers* means (*a*) judgment by those of equal standing (*b*) trial by jury (*c*) judgment by those who look one over thoroughly (*d*) judgment by one's superiors (*e*) judgment by qualified persons.
9. To make a *travesty* of marriage means (*a*) to work out marital problems with a psychiatrist (*b*) to get married after a long journey (*c*) to make marriage an adventure (*d*) to make a mockery of vows taken by not observing them (*e*) to be happily married.
10. A *venal* sin implies (*a*) a social blunder (*b*) a sin committed for money (*c*) an expensive mistake (*d*) a pardonable error (*e*) a sin of the flesh.

11. A *venial* offense is (*a*) easily excused (*b*) unforgivably atrocious (*c*) a first offense (*d*) a civil offense (*e*) an offense of long standing.

B. Match each word in column A with its definition in column B.

Column A	*Column B*
1. laconic	*a.* state of uncontrolled excitement or emotion
2. maudlin	*b.* false
3. sincere	*c.* concise; terse
4. bombast	*d.* worldwide in extent
5. ostracize	*e.* tearfully sentimental
6. delirium	*f.* extravagant speech or writing
7. spurious	*g.* true
8. ecumenical	*h.* universal
9. catholic	*i.* to banish; shut out

C. Using a collegiate dictionary or an unabridged dictionary, look up the etymology and the definition of each of the following words. Then write a brief explanation of how you think each word developed its modern meaning.

1. archaeology
2. ardor
3. arena
4. asinine
5. caricature
6. cloister
7. contaminate
8. curfew

LESSON 4

bane murderer (*n.*)

The Anglo-Saxon word from which we derive the word *bane* is *bana*, meaning "murderer." Hence anything which is your bane is in some way intending to do you harm. Except in the names of poisons such as *ratsbane*, we use the word in a much weaker sense than in the Anglo-Saxon.

bursar purse (*n.*)

The *bursar* is the person who handles financial matters and, in effect, is in charge of the *purse*—the finances of a college, for example.

desultory leaper (*adj.*)

A *desultory* person is, figuratively, a "leaper." He is one who leaps from one subject to another without order or rationale. The word is built on the Latin *de* (down) + salire (to leap).

iconoclast breaker of images (*n.*)

The Greek word for "image" is *eikon* and the Greek for "breaker" is *klastēs*. An *iconoclast* is a figurative "breaker of images"—one who attacks cherished institutions or scorns traditional ideals as being shams. Once a person who literally smashed icons, an iconoclast today is a person who attacks or ridicules anything venerable that he considers to be wrong or superstitious.

innuendo to give a nod (*n.*)

We get this word from the Latin *innuere*, meaning "to give a nod." An *innuendo* is an insinuation both remote and derogatory. It is not an overt act, but rather an allusive one.

propitiate favorable (*v.t.*)

From the Latin *propitius*, meaning "favorable," we derive our word *propitiate*, meaning "to pacify" in lay terms and "to atone for" in theological terms. Since *propitiate* means "to cause to become more favorable, to win, or to regain good will," we use the word most commonly to indicate appeasement or conciliation.

proselyte alien; newcomer (*n.*)

The Greek word *proselytos*, meaning "newcomer" or "alien," comes from two Greek words that literally say, "to come toward." Our most common use of *proselyte*—to denote a person converted to a new religion or political philosophy—is most logical and fitting. If someone says to you, "I am not proselytizing, but —," he means he would like to convert you to his cause, whatever it may be.

stalemate fixed position (*n.*)

From the Anglo-French word *estale*, meaning "a fixed location," we derive the first syllable of the word *stalemate. Mate* comes from the Old French *eschec mat* (checkmate). The Old French is thought to have derived from the Persian *shāh māt*, a phrase meaning "the king is perplexed or dead." This phrase is particularly descriptive because it is applied to a play in chess when the king is rendered unable to move. In chess we have a stalemate when a player cannot move his king without placing the king in check, and there is no other chess piece that can be moved at all. A *stalemate*, therefore, indicates a deadlock because action of any kind is brought to a standstill, checked in a fixed position.

tacit silent (*adj.*)

A *tacit* reply (from the Latin *tacitus*, meaning "silent") might be communicated through a remark in which the reply was implied but not expressed; or it might be communicated through the failure to make any remark at all. In any case the reply itself would be unspoken, unvoiced. A tacit agreement is an unspoken agreement that is reached through a mutual understanding. What is the difference between a tacit communication and an innuendo?

vicarious change; stead (*adj.*)

From the Latin *vicis*, meaning "alteration, change, or stead," we derive our word *vicarious. Vicarious* expresses a substitution, either real or imaginary. If you should ask another person to be a vicarious participant for you at a meeting, for example, you are asking him to take your place. You can enjoy the thrill of shooting an elephant vicariously by substituting yourself in your imagination for the big-game hunter. Arnold Bennett was once severely taken to task by a reader who assumed that the novelist had gone out to witness a hanging just so that he could describe it in his novel *The Old Wives' Tale.* Bennett replied that he had never actually seen a real hanging; he had only read accounts by people who had. In this case Bennett was reporting a vicarious experience and the reader was experiencing her horror third-hand—but still vicariously.

EXERCISES

A. Select the word or phrase that best completes the sentence.

1. To make an *innuendo* is to (*a*) make an entrance (*b*) sing a high note (*c*) make a mistake (*d*) accuse openly (*e*) make an insinuation.
2. *Desultory* means (*a*) lazy (*b*) haphazard (*c*) discontented (*d*) irresponsible (*e*) insulting.
3. To *propitiate* the gods means to (*a*) pray to them (*b*) reject them (*c*) make a bargain with them (*d*) pacify them (*e*) curse them.
4. A *vicarious* experience is an experience that is (*a*) second-hand (*b*) chilling (*c*) religious (*d*) ever-changing (*e*) trying.
5. A *tacit* understanding is (*a*) an agreement in writing (*b*) an agreement reached without words spoken (*c*) an agreement reached after much discussion (*d*) a partial agreement (*e*) a quick agreement.
6. An *iconoclast* is one who (*a*) destroys traditions and conventions (*b*) sets fire to churches (*c*) scolds vociferously (*d*) worships idols (*e*) is in a class by himself.

7. To *proselytize* means (*a*) to try converting people to a cause (*b*) to write in prose (*c*) to be practical (*d*) to heap praise on someone (*e*) to alienate someone.
8. A *stalemate* is (*a*) a technical error (*b*) a boring companion (*c*) a deadlock (*d*) a trap (*e*) a mutual agreement.
9. Today *bane* means (*a*) murderer (*b*) poison (*c*) benefit (*d*) ban (*e*) harm.
10. The *bursar* of a university is concerned with (*a*) campus maintenance (*b*) finances (*c*) the cafeteria (*d*) scholastic records (*e*) honorary degrees.

B. Match each word in column A with its definition in column B.

Column A	*Column B*
1. vixen	*a.* noisy; clamorous
2. peer	*b.* malicious woman
3. blatant	*c.* forgivable
4. venal	*d.* mockery; ridicule
5. venial	*e.* mercenary; done for money
6. travesty	*f.* person equal to another person
7. sinister	*g.* awkward
8. akimbo	*h.* outstandingly bad
9. gauche	*i.* evil
10. gratuitous	*j.* with hands on hips
11. egregious	*k.* freely given

C. Using a collegiate dictionary or an unabridged dictionary, look up the etymology and the definition of each of the following words. Then write a brief explanation of how you think each word developed its modern meaning.

1. demagogue
2. dexterous
3. ecdysiast
4. emaciate
5. exodus
6. expatiate
7. extirpate
8. ptomaine
9. vaccinate

LESSON 5

abyss no bottom (*n.*)

The Greek negative prefix *a* (without) + *byssos* (bottom) compose the English word *abyss*, meaning "a bottomless gulf" or any "deep, immeasurable space." An *abysmal* failure is one who has failed so completely, so miserably, that he has sunk past any measurable stopping place.

acolyte follower (*n.*)

From the Greek *akoulthos*, meaning "follower," we get the English *acolyte*, which means "assistant or helper," most commonly in reference to a boy who serves a priest at Mass.

adroit on the right hand (*adj.*)

Just as *sinister* and *gauche* (Lesson 3) seem to associate some fault or shortcoming with the left side, so *adroit* identifies correctness, ability, skill, with the right side. Since most people are right-handed, the majority has ruled that right is "right." *Adroit* (from the French *droit*, "right") means "dexterous in the use of body or mind." (*Maladroit*, literally, "bad with the right hand," means "awkward, clumsy, inept.")

denouement untie the knot (*n.*)

An author of a play or novel involves his characters in a plot so that he has, in effect, tied a knot. The *denouement* (derived from the Middle French *desnouer*, "to untie") is the conclusion in which the author makes known the outcome of the situations he has created. He has untied the knot that was formed by all the threads of his plot complication.

harridan worn-out horse (*n.*)

If a woman is a vixenish hag, she is a *harridan*. The word is derived from the French word *haridelle*, meaning "worn-out horse or strumpet." The connotation of *harridan* is that of a vicious, scolding woman, usually an old woman.

humor moisture or fluid (*n.*)

In the Middle Ages, before the discovery of the human circulatory system, it was generally believed that the body contained four *humors* or fluids—blood, phlegm, yellow bile, and black bile. These fluids were thought to be responsible for one's disposition, or one's *humor.* For example, a dull, sluggish person was thought to have an oversupply of phlegm in his body. From this we get our word *phlegmatic*, designating either apathy or calmness. The word for black bile comes from the Greek words *melas* (black) + *cholē* (bile). Too much black bile in one's system resulted in *melancholy.* On the other hand, a person who felt cheerful was thought to have a good supply of red blood—hence our word *sanguine* (from Latin *sanguis*, "blood"), meaning "in high, cheerful, healthy spirits." Yellow bile, or choler, was a source of irritability. Consequently a person who was in a bad humor was said to be *choleric.* The theory that there are four humors, or fluids, affecting our dispositions may have been a mistaken one, but perhaps it is not too far removed from the more scientific explanation of glandular secretions which is prevalent today.

iota ninth letter of the Greek alphabet (*n.*)

Iota, the ninth letter of the Greek alphabet, is the smallest letter to be found there. Hence an *iota* in English is "a very small quantity or jot."

platitude flat (*n.*)

The French *plat*, meaning "flat," is the root of the word *platitude.* A platitude is a trite or insipid remark, a truism, a cliché, all of which are certainly *flat* as far as originality of thought and expression are concerned.

procrustean beat out; stretch (*adj.*)

This word means, literally, "inflexible." Its origin goes back to a legendary highwayman of ancient Greece who tied his victims upon an iron bed and either stretched or cut off their legs to adapt the victims to the length of the bed. This highwayman's name, as you have surely guessed, was Procrustes. Today we use the word *procrustean* to designate a point of view that insists upon conformity to a rigid pattern regardless of individual differences.

EXERCISES

A. Select the word or phrase that best completes the sentence.

1. The *denouement* of a novel is (*a*) a synonym for "rising action" (*b*) the climax (*c*) a denunciation of the leading character (*d*) an explanation of the outcome of the plot (*e*) the author's style.
2. *Melancholy* means (*a*) depressed (*b*) mellow (*c*) furious (*d*) sensual (*e*) undecided.
3. A *phlegmatic* person is (*a*) outgoing (*b*) calm (*c*) noisy (*d*) rash (*e*) in bad health.
4. To have not one *iota* of sense means (*a*) to have no sense at all (*b*) to have much good sense (*c*) to have no sensory impairments (*d*) to use a reasonable amount of good judgment (*e*) to make no slips.
5. An *abyss* is (*a*) a deep pool (*b*) a bottomless gulf (*c*) a glacial slide (*d*) a hopeless situation (*e*) a dormant lake.
6. An *acolyte* is a person who (*a*) learns a new skill (*b*) receives an accolade (*c*) acts as an assistant to another (*d*) drinks too much (*e*) does research.
7. A *platitude* is (*a*) a trite remark (*b*) a flat drink (*c*) an original saying (*d*) an insulting remark (*e*) a piece of legislation.
8. To dance *adroitly* means to dance (*a*) clumsily (*b*) on the left foot (*c*) deftly (*d*) continuously (*e*) on the right foot.
9. A *harridan* is (*a*) a two-wheeled coach (*b*) a wool cloak (*c*) a scolding woman (*d*) a dishonest lawyer (*e*) a racehorse.
10. *Procrustean* guidelines would be (*a*) inflexible (*b*) obsolete (*c*) imaginative (*d*) impeccable (*e*) tried and true.

B. Match each word in column A with its definition in column B.

Column A	*Column B*
1. innuendo	*a.* not spoken
2. desultory	*b.* college financial officer
3. bursar	*c.* destroyer of traditional ideas
4. bane	*d.* insinuation
5. propitiate	*e.* disconnected
6. stalemate	*f.* deadlock
7. proselyte	*g.* cause of harm
8. vicarious	*h.* new convert
9. tacit	*i.* to pacify
10. iconoclast	*j.* substitute

C. Using a collegiate dictionary or an unabridged dictionary, look up the etymology and the definition of each of the following words. Then write a brief explanation of how you think each word developed its modern meaning.

1. digit
2. dogma
3. efface
4. equinox
5. etch
6. ethnic
7. excoriate
8. excruciate

LESSON 6

accolade at the neck (*n.*)

The word *accolade* is built on the Latin *collum*, meaning "neck." During the romantic period of history when knights roamed about in quest of deeds of daring, the honor of knighthood was bestowed upon those who performed acts of honor and bravery. Knighthood was conferred upon these individuals by tapping the shoulder just below the neck with a sword. An accolade today is any form of public praise or honor.

affront to strike on the forehead (*n., v.t.*)

Afronter is an Old French word meaning "to strike on the forehead." Hence an *affront* is a personal insult delivered to the face, or right between the eyes. A person may be affronted by words in print, of course, but the insult has much the same effect as if it were a physical attack.

agglomerate to form into a ball (*v.t., v.i.*)

An *agglomeration* of anything is a mass or cluster. The word is built on the Latin *agglomerare*, meaning "to form into a ball."

anthology to gather flowers (*n.*)

Anthos (flower) + *legein* (to gather) form the English word *anthology*—a gathering of the flowers of literature, the passages of literary excellence, into one place. Today any collection of literary works is called an anthology, whether it represents an age, a type, the best of one nationality, or some other unifying theme. We also speak of anthologies of music or of works of art when they are collected together in a book. Obviously the definition of the word has departed somewhat from its original, etymological significance.

assassin hashish (*n.*)

The word *assassin* comes to us from the Arabic language. The Arabic word *hashshāshīn* designates persons who are addicted to hashish, a drug derived from the same hemp plant (*cannabis*) that produces marijuana. The word was extended to become the name of a secret cult. Members of this cult planned murders and committed them while under the influence of drugs. Today an assassin may or may not be influenced by the use of drugs, but the association has certainly not disappeared.

fiasco bottle (*n.*)

A *fiasco* is a completely ridiculous failure. The Venetian glassmaker occasionally turned out a bottle (Italian *fiasco*) that was not of standard quality. The word *fiasco* thus came to designate any undertaking that ended as a ridiculous failure. The plural is *fiascoes.*

gregarious the herd (*adj.*)

If you are a sociable person, one who mixes well in company, you are *gregarious.* In figurative terms, you enjoy being with "the herd" (Latin *grex*, *gregis*). Compare *egregious* in Lesson 3.

obese to eat up (*adj.*)

The Latin *obedere* means "to eat up." People who eat too much may become *obese*, or excessively fat. We have simply transferred the meaning of the word from a cause—(over)eating—to an effect—fatness.

satiate enough (*v.t.*)

When you have *satiated* the palate with sweets, you want no more. You may also satiate the intellect with too much of one kind of mental activity. To be satiated, or *sated*, is to be fully satisfied. Both words, though derived from the Latin *satis*, "enough," may imply overindulgence or excess as well as normal satisfaction.

sophomoric foolishly wise (*adj.*)

From the Greek *sophos* (wise) + *mōros* (foolish) comes this self-contradictory word. The sophists were a group of teacher-philosophers of ancient Greece noted for their clever and skillfully wise arguments. These arguments were often fallacious or specious. The *sophomoric* person is guilty of sophistry: seemingly he knows it all, but in reality he is immature and foolish.

sub rosa under the rose (*adv.*)

The rose is an ancient symbol of secrecy; hence when notables met *under the rose* they were sworn to secrecy. Today the Latin phrase *sub rosa* means "secretly, privately, confidentially."

EXERCISES

A. Select the word or phrase that best completes the sentence.

1. A *gregarious* person is (*a*) an introvert (*b*) an idler (*c*) a farmer (*d*) an extrovert (*e*) a mystic.
2. An *accolade* is (*a*) the granting of a favor (*b*) a series of columns (*c*) the receiving of a gift (*d*) a procession (*e*) the conferring of public praise.
3. An *affront* is (*a*) a compliment (*b*) a pretense (*c*) a complaint (*d*) an insult (*e*) a shield.
4. *Agglomerate* means (*a*) talent (*b*) confusion (*c*) mass (*d*) angle (*e*) noise.
5. A poetry *anthology* is a collection of (*a*) Icelandic sagas (*b*) poetic dictionaries (*c*) selected poems (*d*) verse plays (*e*) words and pictures.
6. A *fiasco* is (*a*) a fiesta (*b*) a fish fry (*c*) a military coup (*d*) a small boat (*e*) a ridiculous failure.
7. *Sophomoric* means (*a*) believing in sophism (*b*) immature (*c*) stupid (*d*) graduating (*e*) philosophical.
8. To be *satiated* with food means (*a*) to be filled (*b*) to be infatuated (*c*) to be nauseated (*d*) to be dissatisfied (*e*) to be tempted.
9. An *assassin* is (*a*) a murderer (*b*) a drug (*c*) a conspirator (*d*) an assistant (*e*) a convict.
10. A meeting held *sub rosa* is conducted (*a*) underground (*b*) in a florist's shop (*c*) in a forest (*d*) in secret (*e*) on the spur of the moment.

11. An *obese* person is excessively (*a*) talkative (*b*) fat (*c*) slow to understand (*d*) stubborn (*e*) melancholy

B. Match each word in column A with its definition in column B.

	Column A		*Column B*
1.	denouement	*a.*	mood; feeling
2.	iota	*b.*	scolding old woman
3.	harridan	*c.*	dexterous; clever
4.	humor	*d.*	trite expression
5.	adroit	*e.*	infinitesimal amount
6.	acolyte	*f.*	assistant
7.	platitude	*g.*	calm
8.	phlegmatic	*h.*	sad
9.	melancholy	*i.*	optimistic
10.	sanguine	*j.*	conclusion of a plot in a novel or play

C. Using a collegiate dictionary or an unabridged dictionary, look up the etymology and the definition of each of the following words. Then write a brief explanation of how you think each word developed its modern meaning.

1. convivial
2. crass
3. cynic
4. debauch
5. deluxe
6. dubious
7. exude
8. mentor
9. neophyte
10. somnambulate

LESSON 7

acronym outermost name (*n.*)

The word *acronym* is derived from the Greek *akros* (highest; extreme; end) + *onyma* (name). Its literal meaning is "name (formed from) extremes (initial letters)." *Acronyms* are words formed from the first (sometimes the first few) letters of several words. RADAR, for example, is formed from *RA*dio *D*etecting *A*nd *R*anging. Other well-known acronyms are CORE, UNESCO, NASA, and WHO (World Health Organization). The formation of acronyms is not peculiar to America alone: *T*elegrafnoe *A*gentstvo *S*ovietskovo *S*oyuza provides the acronym for TASS, the official Soviet news agency. Some parents give their children names whose initials make acronyms. Be careful of this when you are naming your children. What young man wants to have set in diamonds on an 18k gold compact, the initials of a fiancée whose name is *F*ranciola *A*louetta *T*idbit?

amortize death (*v.t.*)

Ad (to) + *mors* (death) make up the word *amortize.* To amortize a debt is to discharge it in advance of maturity by means of a sinking fund. Figuratively speaking, you are putting this debt to death by wiping it out slowly.

billingsgate fish market (*n.*)

Billingsgate was a London fish market noted not only for its piscatorial wares, but also for the vulgar and abusive language used by those who frequented the market. Hence *billingsgate* (with a lower case "b") is foul, abusive, vulgar language.

brogue grip or hold (*n.*)

The word *brogue* is derived from the Irish word *barrog*, meaning "a grip or hold." Actually the grip or hold referred to is on the tongue. Once the Irish language grips the tongue, it seems never to quite relinquish its hold. More than other speech habits, the brogue of the Irish persists in manifesting itself even when the speaker communicates in some other dialect or tongue. Do not confuse *brogue* used in this sense with the noun *brogue* meaning "a heavy, comfortable shoe." To find a metaphoric relationship between an Irish brogue fitting the tongue as comfortably as a friendly old shoe fits the foot is probably pure Irish fantasy.

didactic apt at teaching (*adj.*)

In its sense of "intended for instruction," *didactic* is not far removed from its etymological origin in the Greek *didaskein*, "to teach." The connotation that has attached itself to *didactic*, however, gives the word an unpleasant flavor. We associate the word *didactic* with one who is *too much* inclined to teach others (often, unfortunately, a school teacher), insisting always on belaboring the morally instructive aspects of any learning.

effete exhausted (*adj.*)

This word comes to English via the Latin word *effetus*, which is a compound of *ex* (out) + *fetus* (childbearing). Although *effetus* can be translated to mean "that has brought forth," it was also used to describe a woman "worn out by childbearing." Our word *effete*, meaning "exhausted of fertility," usually applies to conditions other than the fruitfulness of women. For example, a civilization which is dying is referred to as an effete culture.

holocaust whole burned (*n.*)

Holocaust means "complete destruction by fire." The Greek *holos* (whole) + *kaustos* (burned) are the elements from which the English word is derived. Originally the word meant a sacrificial offering the whole of which was consumed in fire.

jargon chattering; warbling (*n.*)

Derived from the Old French *gargon*, meaning "a chattering," this word today means more specifically "confused, unintelligible language; gibberish." It is also applied to a technical or secret vocabulary of a particular science, art, or subculture understood only by those who are within the group.

obsequious to comply with (*adj.*)

Once used to mean "devoted or dutiful," our word *obsequious* (from the Latin *obsequiosus*, "compliant") now describes a person excessively willing to obey or overly servile. Is a sycophant likely to be obsequious?

tawdry corruption of *St. Audrey* (*adj.*)

Neckpieces known as St. Audrey's laces (bought at the Fair of St. Audrey) became *tawdry* laces. Today the word means "showy, tasteless, cheap."

vapid insipid; stale (*adj.*)

Coming from the Latin adjective *vapidus*, meaning "stale" or "insipid," the word *vapid* describes a person, a conversation, or a piece of writing that is dull and unexciting.

EXERCISES

A. Select the word or phrase that best completes the sentence.

1. To *amortize* means (*a*) to kill (*b*) to provide for gradual payment of a debt (*c*) to invest in mutual funds (*d*) to postpone (*e*) to put up for auction.
2. *Billingsgate* is (*a*) a fishmonger (*b*) a London prison (*c*) a picket fence (*d*) coarse, abusive language (*e*) a dialect of English.
3. To be *didactic* is to be (*a*) a school teacher (*b*) informal (*c*) ridiculous (*d*) ironic (*e*) overly moralistic.
4. The word *brogue* is usually associated with (*a*) rough behavior (*b*) a speech impediment (*c*) an Irish dialect (*d*) a French accent (*e*) cosmetics.

5. An *acronym* is (*a*) a word formed from the first letters of several words (*b*) a pen name (*c*) a word used as a synonym for another word (*d*) a word used as an antonym of another word (*e*) a word used in overstatement.
6. *Effete* means (*a*) efficacious (*b*) effeminate (*c*) exhausted (*d*) efficient (*e*) gigantic.
7. A *holocaust* is (*a*) complete destruction by fire (*b*) a whole cause (*c*) a corpse full of holes (*d*) a predicament (*e*) a bankruptcy.
8. *Jargon* is (*a*) a cracked vase (*b*) a chemical element (*c*) a classical Oriental language (*d*) unintelligible language (*e*) a kind of seaweed.
9. An *obsequious* person is (*a*) overly servile (*b*) overweight (*c*) obsolete (*d*) secretive (*e*) a cult follower.
10. A *vapid* smile is (*a*) seductive (*b*) bilious (*c*) insipid (*d*) inspiring (*e*) vanishing.
11. *Tawdry* jewelry is showy and (*a*) expensive (*b*) colorful (*c*) theatrical (*d*) cheap (*e*) unusual.

B. Match each word in column A with its definition in column B.

Column A	*Column B*
1. gregarious	*a.* very fat
2. accolade	*b.* killer
3. affront	*c.* personal insult
4. agglomerate	*d.* public honor
5. anthology	*e.* ridiculous failure
6. fiasco	*f.* social
7. sophomoric	*g.* secretly
8. obese	*h.* completely satisfied
9. assassin	*i.* to gather into a cluster
10. satiated	*j.* collection of selected literary pieces
11. sub rosa	*k.* immature

C. Using a collegiate dictionary or an unabridged dictionary, look up the etymology and the definition of each of the following words. Then write a brief explanation of how you think each word developed its modern meaning.

1. argosy
2. assuage
3. asylum
4. banal
5. Bible
6. bonbon
7. companion
8. equivocal
9. gland
10. obsequies
11. October
12. pedantic

LESSON 8

bucolic herdsman; cowherd (*adj.*)

Bucolic is built on the Greek *boukolos*, meaning "herdsman" or "cowherd." Herdsmen and cowherds are usually associated with rural or countrified life; hence *bucolic* in English means "pastoral; rustic; pertaining to farm life."

canard duck (*n.*)

A *canard* in English is a false or unfounded story. The fact that this meaning has developed from the French word for "duck" is indeed curious. Etymologists trace the term to a French expression which translates literally "to half-sell ducks." We picture a situation where ducks were offered for sale without actually being produced, the implication being that they never existed in the first place. The offer for sale of the nonexistent ducks created the impression that there were ducks to sell. Similarly a *canard* makes assertions or implications that seem credible because of the way they are presented, but actually are untrue.

curate to take care of (*n.*)

The Latin word *curare* means "to take care of," and from this word we get *curate.* A curate specifically takes care of souls, endeavoring to get them to Heaven. The head of a museum is called a *curator.* Do you see why?

genuflect to bend the knee (*v.i.*)

Genu is the Latin word for "knee" and *flectere* means "to bend." When a person *genuflects* in his place of worship, he bends his knee in reverential respect to the altar and all that it signifies.

grovel on the face; prone (*v.i.*)

The Middle English word *grufeling*, meaning "prone," provides the origin of this word. *Grovel* means "to lie prone" in the sense that one would crawl in abject servitude. It is a word that might aptly be applied to a sycophant.

mellifluous to flow with honey (*adj.*)

Sounds are considered to be *mellifluous* if they are especially "sweet" and "pleasant to the ear." The human voice is often referred to as being mellifluous if its tone is rich and dulcet. Derived from the Latin *mellis* (honey) + *fluere* (to flow), the word *mellifluous* itself has the sound of honey.

mollify to make soft (*v.t.*)

Mollis (soft) + *ficare* (to make) are the Latin elements which make the word *mollify*, meaning "to appease or mitigate." You would certainly do everything in your power to mollify an irate policeman who was deciding whether or not to write you a summons for reckless driving.

monolithic composed of a single stone (*adj.*)

Monolithic is derived from two Greek words which appear in the etymology of many English words—*monos* (single) and *lithos* (stone). Many obelisks of ancient Egypt were monolithic in both form and structure; that is, they were composed of a single, solid stone. The Washington Monument is monolithic in form only, for it has a hollow structure. The term *monolithic* has been extended to describe anything that is one massive, undifferentiated whole, exhibiting solid conformity and one harmonious pattern throughout. The Catholic Church has been called a monolithic organization, as has the Communist Party.

obelisk pointed pillar (*n.*)

An *obelisk* is a four-sided monolithic ("one-stone") pillar, tapering as it rises and terminating in a pyramid; it is also a mark of reference (an inverted spit or dagger †) found in textbooks. The Washington Monument has the form of an obelisk but is not composed of a single stone. Examples of true obelisks are the obelisk in the Place de la Concorde in Paris and Cleopatra's Needle in New York.

procrastinate tomorrow (*v.i.*)

For *procrastinators* tomorrow never comes. They habitually defer or postpone things which should be done now; hence the famous adage, "Procrastination is the thief of time." The word *procrastinate* says what it means, for it is derived from the Latin *pro* (forward) + *crastinus* (tomorrow).

saturnine born under the influence of the planet Saturn (*adj.*)

The planet Saturn is associated in astrology with the metal lead. A person born under this planet is said to be basically gloomy and taciturn; hence our word *saturnine*, meaning "sluggish, gloomy, or sullen." The association of the metal lead with heaviness and dullness may help you to remember the meaning of *saturnine*.

symposium drinking party (*n.*)

Sym (with) + *posis* (drinking) are the Greek word elements forming the English word *symposium*. Today a symposium is a conference at which a particular subject is discussed by a panel of experts. Usually at the symposium itself nothing stronger than black coffee is served. Since some people regard drinking as a serious business and since many are able to discourse on intellectual subjects more fluently when relaxed by alcohol, our meaning of the word may be quite logical.

EXERCISES

A. Select the sentence in which the italicized word is used correctly.

1. *a.* She admired the sophisticated man-about-town for his *bucolic* table manners.
   b. I love New York because of its teeming, *bucolic* streets.
   c. Sheep grazing, cows lowing, dogs quietly watching created a scene of halcyon, *bucolic* loveliness.
2. *a.* All doctors are *curates*.
   b. The *curate* visited his parishioners once a week.
   c. A *curate* must be able to pass the bar exams.
3. *a.* To *genuflect* is to do a noble deed.
   b. One is expected to *genuflect* when presented to the Queen of England.
   c. One is required to *genuflect* in the presence of the President of the United States of America.

4. *a.* Patrick Henry would *grovel* in the dust for no English king.
   b. He showed his fierce spirit of independence by *groveling* before the conqueror.
   c. "Stand up and *grovel!*" roared the Captain.

5. *a.* A *procrastinator* is a person who tells little white lies.
   b. He who *procrastinates* today will have twice as much to do tomorrow.
   c. His friends called him a *procrastinator* because he always did tomorrow's homework as soon as the class was dismissed.

6. *a.* Automobile design has been *mollified* in recent years.
   b. He will *mollify* your bank statement for income tax purposes.
   c. A bouquet of long-stemmed roses has been known to *mollify* an angry wife.

7. *a.* The whole group was feeling *saturnine* because of the beautiful spring weather.
   b. Father's *saturnine* mood served to discourage conversation at supper.
   c. He had such *saturnine* virtues as courage, patience, and foresight.

8. *a.* Orange blossom honey has a characteristic *mellifluous* flavor.
   b. The *mellifluous* millionaire left all his money to charity.
   c. I fell asleep in a meadow filled with *mellifluous* murmurings.

9. *a.* Edward's determination was such that no *obelisk* could stop him.
   b. Egyptian pharoahs were buried in ornate *obelisks.*
   c. Two slender *obelisks* stood at either side of the entrance to the temple.

10. *a.* He spoke quietly in a *monolithic* tone of voice.
    b. The young man took a vow of eternal silence when he joined the small, *monolithic* order of recluse monks.
    c. The saber-toothed tiger became extinct in the *monolithic* era.

11. *a.* The annual track and field championships were held in the newly constructed *symposium.*

b. A *symposium* of educators met to discuss changes in the science curriculum.
c. Bach composed music for the *symposium* and the harpsichord.

12. *a.* The *canard* was singing joyfully in its cage.
b. The ballyhoo of the carnival huckster was pure *canard.*
c. We played four-handed *canard* until Blackjack Peabody won the game.

B. Match each word in column A with its definition in column B.

Column A	*Column B*
1. amortize	*a.* abusive language
2. billingsgate	*b.* worn out
3. brogue	*c.* regional dialect
4. effete	*d.* confused language
5. jargon	*e.* moralistic
6. didactic	*f.* name formed with initial letters of words
7. vapid	*g.* insipid
8. obsequious	*h.* complete destruction
9. tawdry	*i.* fawning
10. acronym	*j.* to repay a debt before its due date over a period of time
11. holocaust	*k.* cheap, showy

C. Using a collegiate dictionary or an unabridged dictionary, look up the etymology and the definition of each of the following words. Then write a brief explanation of how you think each word developed its modern meaning.

1. blanch
2. carte blanche
3. caste
4. caustic
5. cemetery
6. certificate
7. church
8. insipid

LESSON 9

adumbrate to shade (*v.t.*)

From the Latin *ad* (to) + *umbra* (shade) comes our word *adumbrate*, meaning "to outline faintly," "to sketch in a shadowy way," or "to foreshadow." Think of some other "shady" words in English, such as *umbrella, umbrage, umber.* Any others?

emancipate to take out of the hand (*v.t.*)

The Latin *e* (out of) + *manus* (hand) + *capere* (to take) form the English word *emancipate.* To *emancipate* means, literally, "to take out of the hand," or, in its modern definition, "to set free." Thus in emancipating the slaves, Lincoln took them out of the hands of their former masters.

halcyon kingfisher (*adj.*)

The Greek *hals* (sea) + *kyōn* (kingfisher) give our word *halcyon* a most romantic origin. According to ancient legend, the kingfisher hatched its young in a nest that floated on the seas at the time of the winter solstice. In order that the eggs hatch without danger, the kingfisher supposedly calmed the seas at this period of the year. From this legend is derived our word halcyon, meaning "calm, peaceful, happy, golden, or prosperous."

hyperbole an overshooting (*n.*)

Hyperbole is a rhetorical device expressing an obvious exaggeration to create a desired effect. "He was as strong as a lion" is an example of hyperbole. The word's definition is graphically expressed by its etymology: Greek *hyper* (over) + *ballein* (to throw). The opposite literary device, understatement, is called *litotes.*

lachrymal a tear (*adj.*)

The Latin word *lacrima* means "a tear (teardrop)." The *lachrymal* glands in the eyes are responsible for your being able to shed tears. A meeting at which there is much weeping would be a lachrymal occasion. A person who sheds tears easily is called *lachrymose*. The words may also be spelled *lacrimal* and *lacrimose*.

piquant to prick or sting (*adj.*)

The French *piquer*, meaning "to prick or sting," gives us the word *piquant*, meaning "pleasantly tart, sharp, biting, pungent." A young lady who is piquant is therefore stimulating and provocative. The noun *pique* comes from exactly the same French word, but means "resentment at being stung by having someone slight you or offend you."

pogrom devastation (*n.*)

This word is derived from Yiddish, the language of Eastern European Jews. An often-persecuted minority in Russia, the Jews there borrowed the Russian word for "devastation"—*pogrom*—and gave it the meaning it now has in English: "an organized massacre of defenseless people." Notorious pogroms have been those perpetrated by the czarist government against the Jews in Russia and by Hitler against the Jews in Germany and throughout Europe.

poignant to sting (*adj.*)

Derived from the Old French *poindre*, meaning "to sting," the English word *poignant* means "painfully moving" or "piercingly effective." We often use the word to describe a touching novel or movie or some news story that affects us emotionally. In a figurative sense, it is your heart which is stung by a poignant incident.

polemic warlike (*n.*)

Polemic is the art of controversy. A *polemic* can designate either an aggressive controversialist or the attack made by him. The word comes from the Greek *polemos*, meaning "war."

salubrious health (*adj.*)

The Latin *salus* means "health"; thus a *salubrious* climate or a salubrious diet is a healthful one. The word *salutary* comes from the same root as *salubrious*, but expresses the idea of effecting, or being designed to bring about, improvement. *Salubrious* indicates a healthful or beneficial condition; *salutary* suggests the correcting or preventing of an unhealthy or harmful condition. Salutary advice, for example, is the kind given to you "for your own good."

solecism speaking incorrectly (*n.*)

The colonists in Soloi spoke a corrupt form of Attic, a dialect of ancient Greek. A *solecism* is hence a violation of the grammar or conventional usage of a language. A substandard expression such as "I seen him" is a solecism.

tautology same word (*n.*)

Tautology is built on the Greek words *tauto* (same) + *logos* (word) and means "a redundancy" or "a needless repetition." A frequently used tautological expression is "mental telepathy." It is quite impossible to define the word "telepathy" without using the word "mental" either explicitly or implicitly; hence the word "mental" in the phrase is tautological. Think of some other examples of your own—"necessary essentials," "small little house," and so on.

EXERCISES

A. Select the sentence in which the italicized word is used correctly.

1. *a.* I cried over the *poignant* love scene in the story.
   b. He stabbed me with a *poignant* dagger.
   c. Be still, my *poignant* heart.
2. *a.* The climate was *salubrious.*
   b. Your *salubrious* apology is accepted.
   c. When we win the prize, we'll all *salubriate.*
3. *a.* He beat a *halcyon* tattoo on the drums.
   b. The bird hatched a *halcyon* egg.
   c. I dream of *halcyon* days to come after I retire from this frantic job.
4. *a.* I have some medicine that is good for *emancipation.*
   b. Susan B. Anthony crusaded for the *emancipation* of women.
   c. I came to this conclusion only after great *emancipation.*
5. *a.* There must be some *hyperbole* to this dilemma.

   b. We rarely understood the professor because he always spoke in *hyperboles.*
   c. If I can't understand a simple *hyperbole,* how can I ever do calculus?

6. *a.* A knowledge of *tautology* is essential for a marine navigator.
   b. "Bring all essential necessities" is a *tautological* command.
   c. *Tautology* is included in the list of courses taught in the philosophy department.

7. *a.* It was a *lachrymal* occasion when the children buried the dead bird.
   b. A *lachrymal* person is lacking in sentiment.
   c. The sky was bright and *lachrymal.*

8. *a.* This jewelry isn't worth a *piquant.*
   b. A *piquant* woman is always picking at trifles.
   c. The girl had a lively, *piquant* quality.

9. *a.* The ambassador's *polemic* attitude reassured us of his sincere wish for peace.
   b. The dictator delivered such a *polemic* against them that the democracies of the world were frightened.
   c. He maintained good *polemics* with his neighbors.

10. *a.* The tyrant instituted a *pogrom* against the original inhabitants of the country.
    b. A *pogrom* is beneficial to every person included in it.
    c. Lincoln advocated a *pogrom* for the slaves.

11. *a.* The strike was *adumbrated* by a series of fruitless negotiations.
    b. When Vincent's old car became *adumbrated,* he decided to trade it for a new model.
    c. The teacher returned Henry's paper with the comment that it was too long and should be *adumbrated.*

12. *a.* Lucille's *solecism* "He don't know nothing" horrified the English professor.
    b. It's small *solecism* to lock the garage door after the car has been stolen.
    c. He was honored for his wit, *solecism,* and wisdom.

B. Match each word in column A with its definition in column B.

Column A	*Column B*
1. bucolic	*a.* to delay
2. canard	*b.* massive
3. curate	*c.* to crawl abjectly
4. genuflect	*d.* conference
5. saturnine	*e.* unfounded report
6. grovel	*f.* to bend the knee
7. monolithic	*g.* rustic
8. procrastinate	*h.* gloomy
9. mellifluous	*i.* stone column
10. mollify	*j.* clergyman
11. symposium	*k.* sweet-sounding
12. obelisk	*l.* to appease

C. Using a collegiate dictionary or an unabridged dictionary, look up the etymology and the definition of each of the following words. Then write a brief explanation of how you think each word developed its modern meaning.

1. cogent
2. cognizance
3. commemorate
4. compendium
5. conciliate
6. concoct
7. congeal
8. hoarse
9. kismet
10. turnpike

LESSON 10

anathema thing devoted to evil (*n.*)

Derived from the Greek *anatithenai*, meaning "to set up or dedicate," the word *anathema* denotes a thing dedicated to evil. An anathema is a ban or curse, often ecclesiastical in nature, but not necessarily. Matthew Maule in *The House of the Seven Gables* called down anathema on the Pyncheon family. We also use the word to denote an object of intense dislike. Thus a person who has been ostracized from a group might be considered anathema by the members of the group; a particular school subject might be anathema to a student.

deride to laugh in a bad sense (*v.t.*)

The Latin *deridēre* is composed of two other words, *de* (giving bad sense to the verb) + *ridēre* (to laugh). The English word *derisive* thus implies the laughter of ridicule rather than the healthy laughter of enjoyment. *Derision* is the wilting laughter of scorn and contempt, and one who derides another is laughing at him, not with him.

heinous to hate (*adj.*)

Heinous is a word reserved for the most evil of deeds. It comes to English via the Middle French *haineus*, from *haine*, meaning "hate." Abominations such as fratricide or the outrages committed under the Nazi regime are heinous deeds.

impugn to fight (*v.t.*)

The word *impugn*, from the Latin words *in* (against) + *pugnare* (to fight), means, not to engage in actual physical combat, but to attack by argument or to challenge something as false. The word implies verbal combat.

persiflage whistle; hiss; boo (*n.*)

Persiflage is a lightly derisive manner of treating a subject. Derived from the French *per* (thoroughly) + *siffler* (to hiss or whistle), the word rather logically comes to mean "banter" or "a frivolous style of writing or speaking."

sardonic bitter (*adj.*)

The word *sardonic* means "scornful, cynical, or bitterly mocking." We speak of a sardonic attitude toward life, a sardonic drama review, a sardonic comment. The word is probably derived from the Latin *Sardonius* (*rīsus*), "bitter (laugh)," a meaning which supposedly came from *herba Sardonia*, or "Sardinian herb." This herb was poisonous and, if eaten, caused the face of the eater to become distorted. In time the combination of the name Sardonia and the painful grimace caused by the herb came to indicate a bitter expression (or laugh) and eventually broadened to describe bitterness or cynicism in general.

scintillate spark (*v.i.*)

The Latin word *scintilla* means "a spark." From that noun comes our word *scintillate*, meaning "to emit quick flashes as if throwing off sparks." We apply the word to something that sparkles literally, like fireworks, or figuratively, like a bright eye or a witty remark.

stigma the prick or mark of a pointed instrument (*n.*)

The word *stigma* comes from the Greek *stigmatos*, meaning "a mark or brand." A person who is *stigmatized*, or carries a stigma, is marked in some way in a negative sense. The stigma identifies the person as one who is guilty of wrongdoing or dishonor. The word *stigmata* (the plural of *stigma*) has acquired a very different sense through its association with the marks on Christ's hands and feet left by the nails which fastened him to the cross.

stratagem a general (*n.*)

The Greek word *stratēgos* means "a general," and from it we get the word *stratagem*, "a trick used in war to fool the enemy." In popular usage, a stratagem is a deception or a ruse. One of the most famous tricks of this type was the legendary wooden horse filled with Greek warriors that was accepted as a gift by the gullible Trojans.

suborn to furnish secretly (*v.t.*)

To *suborn* is to induce secretly the commission of an unlawful act. For example, should a lawyer induce a witness to give false testimony and thus commit perjury, this testimony has been suborned, or if a person is bribed to falsify the truth, the person has been suborned. The word comes from the Latin *sub* (secretly) + *ornare* (to furnish).

EXERCISES

A. Select the word or phrase that best completes the sentence.

1. *Sardonic* implies (*a*) bitter mockery (*b*) grim tragedy (*c*) light-hearted humor (*d*) carelessness (*e*) deception.
2. A *stigma* is (*a*) a tumor (*b*) a handicap (*c*) an eye imperfection (*d*) a superstition (*e*) a mark of shame.
3. An *anathema* is (*a*) a natural catastrophe (*b*) a game of anagrams (*c*) a puzzle (*d*) a curse (*e*) a musical composition.
4. Something *scintillating* is (*a*) wicked (*b*) sparkling (*c*) hot (*d*) sinful (*e*) exciting.
5. To *impugn* means (*a*) to attack with words (*b*) to honor (*c*) to reject (*d*) to excuse (*e*) to question.
6. *Persiflage* is (*a*) perjury (*b*) derisive banter (*c*) destructive behavior (*d*) grave peril (*e*) angry speech.
7. To *suborn* means (*a*) to subordinate (*b*) to undercut (*c*) to furnish secretly (*d*) to be born again (*e*) to supplement.
8. A *stratagem* is (*a*) a top-ranking military man (*b*) a tricky maneuver (*c*) a geological stratum (*d*) a rare jewel (*e*) a striated surface.
9. A *heinous* deed is (*a*) wicked (*b*) foolish (*c*) accidental (*d*) courageous (*e*) secret.

10. To *deride* a suggestion is to (*a*) praise it (*b*) derive benefit from it (*c*) make fun of it (*d*) override it (*e*) take a vote on it.

B. Match each word in column A with its definition in column B.

Column A	*Column B*
1. poignant	*a.* redundancy
2. emancipate	*b.* overstatement
3. hyperbole	*c.* healthful
4. tautology	*d.* misuse of a word
5. lachrymal	*e.* to foreshadow
6. piquant	*f.* tearful
7. polemic	*g.* peaceful
8. halcyon	*h.* provocative
9. adumbrate	*i.* organized massacre of civilians
10. solecism	*j.* deeply affecting
11. salubrious	*k.* to set free
12. pogrom	*l.* warlike speech or writing

C. Using a collegiate dictionary or an unabridged dictionary, look up the etymology and the definition of each of the following words. Then write a brief explanation of how you think each word developed its modern meaning.

1. consolidate
2. contemporary
3. hoax
4. leech
5. lettuce
6. sarcasm
7. stomach
8. succotash

LESSON 11

galaxy milk (*n.*)

The sense of "milk" in the Greek word *gala* carries over into the English word *galaxy*. One well-known galaxy, that brilliant band of light we call the Milky Way, is made up of so many millions of stars that a milky effect is visible to the naked eye. The word *galaxy* is also used to mean a congregation of brilliant people or a brilliant array of things.

hell to cover; hide (*n.*)

Like the word *iniquity*, the word *hell* seems to have taken on the terrifying characteristics now associated with it only in Anglo-Saxon times. In fact, the word never appears in the Old Testament at all, nor were the ancient Jews concerned especially with everlasting life, either halcyon or horrible. Possibly derived from *Hel*, the name of the Norse goddess of death, or from the Old High German *helan*, "to conceal," the word *hell* became the Christian synonym for the place of eternal damnation and suffering reserved for those who died with iniquitous deeds upon their hands and hearts. The Greek Hades was a nether-world of shade and sorrow, but not the place of fire and torment that *hell* became in Christian theology and literature.

incline to lean (*v.t.*, *v.i.*)

Our word *incline* is not too far removed in meaning from its Latin sources *in* (to; toward) + *clinare* (to lean). We use the word in many colorful senses. As a transitive verb, we use the word *incline* in the sense of "to make willing" or "to influence," as well as in the more literal sense of "to bend." A vivid use of the word in the latter sense is the supplication to God, "Incline thine ear to us." Closely associated with *clivus* (hill) in the sense of a leaning, sloping, or slanting is our word *inclination*, denoting a particular disposition or bent toward something, a preference, or a bending of the body or head as in bowing. *Inclination* in the sense of "preference" or "bent" has a much more positive connotation than *proclivity* (see below, this lesson).

iniquity uneven (*n.*)

Derived from the same Latin words as the word *inequity—in* (not) + *aequus* (equal or level)—the word *iniquity* somewhere underwent a change, possibly in the Middle English, and took on a very strong meaning. Rather than indicating injustice or unfairness as *inequity* does, the word *iniquity* means an injustice so gross that it is wicked. Consequently an iniquitous act is a sinful act.

proclivity sloping forward (*n.*)

A *proclivity* indicates a strong inclination toward something. Derived from the Latin *pro* (forward) + *clivus* (hill), the word implies a strong inclination toward something objectionable or undesirable. We may speak either of a proclivity *to something*, as a proclivity *to gambling*; or a proclivity *to do something*, as a proclivity *to gamble.*

quixotic Don Quixote (*adj.*)

Don Quixote (in Spanish pronounced kee-'ho-tay) was the impractical, idealistic hero of the novel written by Cervantes in the early 17th century. Appalled by the poverty, starvation, and injustice that he saw all around him, Cervantes created Don Quixote (rhymes in English with "fix it") to satirize a society that had no ideals, no gallantry, no compassion, no honor. Thus into our language comes the word *quixotic*, meaning "impractically idealistic or foolishly chivalrous." When we say that someone is the kind of person who would fight windmills, we are referring to one of the Don's misadventures in his gallant crusade to restore to the world some measure of honor.

sabbath cease from (*n.*)

The Hebrew verb *shabeth* means "to cease from or rest." We have extended that meaning in our word *sabbath.* Today *Sabbath* (usually capitalized) means a day on which we cease from doing routine activities. The Sabbath of the Jews and the Seventh Day Adventists is the seventh day of the week, or our calendar Saturday. For most Christian churches, Sunday, technically the first day of the week, is regarded as the Sabbath. Also derived from the Hebrew *shabeth* is our word *sabbatical,* which denotes a year of rest at regular intervals, originally every seventh year as designated by Mosaic law for resting the fields and vineyards and releasing debtors from their obligations.

supercilious raised eyebrow (*adj.*)

The Latin word *cilium* means "eyelid" or "the region of the eyebrow." *Super,* of course, means "over or above." A supercilious person is one who shows his arrogant doubt of your intelligence by either literally or figuratively "raising an eyebrow" at some remark you may make. Not particularly comfortable to have around, supercilious people are haughtily proud or scornful and impugn the knowledge of others by this simple, but shattering, facial movement.

superfluous to flow over (*adj.*)

Superfluous, derived from *super* (over) + *fluere* (to flow), means "more than enough" in the sense that anything overflowing does not need more added. To add more coffee to a cup already spilling over onto one's best suit would be to add superfluous liquid. A superfluous remark is one that is not needed. Notice the pronunciation of this word. Usually *super* accents the first syllable, either with primary stress, as in *supermarket,* or with secondary stress, as in *supercilious.* In *superfluous,* however, the accent is on the second syllable. If you mispronounce this word, someone is likely to make a derisive comment about your ignorance, or raise a supercilious brow.

supplant under the sole of the foot (*v.t.*)

Were we to *supplant* our form of democracy with a dictatorship, we would figuratively step on the concept of democracy and wipe it out. The Latin source of this word captures the idea of "stamping out": *sub* (under) + *planta* (sole of the foot). To *supplant* means "to replace a person, an institution, or an idea, usually by force."

EXERCISES

A. Select the word or phrase that best completes the sentence.

1. A *supercilious* person is (*a*) middle-aged (*b*) tense (*c*) arrogant (*d*) comfortable (*e*) talkative.
2. *Superfluous* means (*a*) more than necessary (*b*) powerful (*c*) proud (*d*) extravagant (*e*) rapid.
3. To *supplant* means (*a*) to challenge (*b*) to eradicate and replace (*c*) to support (*d*) to plant again (*e*) to hide.
4. An example of a *galaxy* is (*a*) the moon (*b*) Venus (*c*) the Milky Way (*d*) the solar system (*e*) the universe.
5. *Proclivity* means (*a*) leaning over backwards (*b*) evil intentions (*c*) sharp angle (*d*) predisposition toward something objectionable (*e*) dangerous position.
6. To have an *inclination* toward something is to have (*a*) an obsession (*b*) a preference (*c*) a hatred (*d*) an opinion (*e*) an allergy.
7. An *iniquitous* deed is (*a*) wicked (*b*) unfair (*c*) illegal (*d*) questionable (*e*) ineffective.
8. A *quixotic* person is (*a*) moronic (*b*) impractically idealistic (*c*) impossibly quizzical (*d*) unconventional (*e*) hasty.
9. *Sabbath* is a word for (*a*) every seventh year (*b*) a place of worship (*c*) a book of scriptures (*d*) a day of rest occurring once a week (*e*) a feast lasting seven days.

B. Match each word in column A with its definition in column B.

	Column A		*Column B*
1.	sardonic	*a.*	curse
2.	stigma	*b.*	clever trick or ruse
3.	stratagem	*c.*	abominable
4.	suborn	*d.*	mark of shame
5.	heinous	*e.*	to ridicule
6.	anathema	*f.*	to sparkle
7.	impugn	*g.*	to attack with words
8.	persiflage	*h.*	sarcastic
9.	deride	*i.*	to furnish secretly
10.	scintillate	*j.*	banter

C. Using a collegiate dictionary or an unabridged dictionary, look up the etymology and the definition of each of the following words. Then write a brief explanation of how you think each word developed its modern meaning.

1. athlete
2. aura
3. cabal
4. cascade
5. catharsis
6. compromise
7. environment
8. epicure
9. generic

LESSON 12

bellicose war (*adj.*)

Bellum is the Latin word for "war," and from it we get the word *bellicose*, meaning "warlike." Nations often assume a bellicose attitude in their foreign policy. An individual may become bellicose if he "has a chip on his shoulder" and is looking for a fight. Compare the etymology of *bellicose* with that of the word *polemic* (page 39).

coquette to strut like a rooster (*n.*)

Coquette is the feminine form of the French word *coquet*, which originally described a man who tried to attract attention or admiration by his elegant clothing or his elegant manners. *Coquet* is the diminutive form of the French word *coq*, meaning "rooster." We use the word *coquette* entirely in application to women, indicating a woman who is a flirt. If you have ever seen a rooster preening and parading before his barnyard harem, you will recognize the aptness of the comparison to a flirtatious female.

hiatus to yawn (*n.*)

The past participle of the Latin *hiare*, "to yawn," becomes our word *hiatus*, denoting a break in the continuity or a gap where something is missing.

mercenary wages; reward (*n.*, *adj.*)

A *mercenary* is one who will fight, do the work of a spy and an informer, or even turn traitor—all for money or some other material reward. It matters not to the mercenary what principles are involved if he gets paid (Latin *merces*, "wages"). This meaning of *mercenary* applies to the noun—the person himself. The adjective *mercenary* characterizes such a person, his work, or his motive.

myriad ten thousand (*n.*, *adj.*)

In English the word *myriad* means "countless" or "innumerable." It is built on the Greek *myrioi*, meaning "ten thousand." Ten thousand is by no means countless, but it is a substantial number—especially if you are counting beans, blades of grass, stars, or other objects occurring in great numbers and difficult to count precisely.

onerous a load (*adj.*)

The Latin *onus* means, literally, "a load." We use the word *onerous* to describe anything "burdensome" or "laborious," although we are not usually talking about physical labor. *Onerous* is more apt to be used to describe duties that are annoying or tedious than ones that are impossibly strenuous.

peninsula almost an island (*n.*)

The Latin *paene* (almost) + *insula* (island) combine to form our word *peninsula*: a piece of land nearly surrounded by water.

prevaricate to walk crookedly (*v.i.*)

Derived from the Latin *prae* (before) + *varicare* (to straddle), the word *prevaricate* means "to be guilty of a 'slight' falsehood or clouding of the truth." That definition might be considered euphemistic; is half a lie a lie? Gertrude Stein would say that a lie is a lie is a lie . . . .

prosthesis an addition (*n.*)

Derived from the Greek *pros* (to) + *tithenai* (to place), the word *prosthetics* identifies the branch of surgery that adds an artificial part to the body. A *prosthesis* is an artificial device added to the body where a part is damaged or missing.

supplicate to bend (*v.t.*, *v.i.*)

The Latin *sub* (under) + *plicare* (to fold) make our word *supplicate*, which means "to make humble entreaty" or "to implore on bended knee."

EXERCISES

A. Select the word or phrase that best completes the sentence.

1. A *coquette* is (*a*) a flirtatious woman (*b*) a dessert (*c*) a rooster (*d*) a dancer (*e*) a ridiculous failure.

2. To be *bellicose* is to be (*a*) obese (*b*) conceited (*c*) argumentative (*d*) beautiful (*e*) friendly.

3. *Myriad* means (*a*) a countless number (*b*) a miraculous occurrence (*c*) a mythological tale (*d*) transparent (*e*) microscopic.

4. A *mercenary* is (*a*) a slave (*b*) a mercurial person (*c*) a benefactor (*d*) a hired soldier (*e*) a treasurer.

5. A *prevarication* is (*a*) a little white lie (*b*) a false accusation (*c*) a perverted idea (*d*) an unsuccessful attempt (*e*) a warning.

6. A *supplication* is (*a*) a curse (*b*) a humble plea (*c*) an addition (*d*) an impatient demand (*e*) a reply.

7. A *hiatus* is (*a*) a continuity (*b*) a break in continuity (*c*) an eternity (*d*) a loud cry (*e*) a false start.

8. *Onerous* means (*a*) repulsive (*b*) burdensome (*c*) possessive (*d*) singular (*e*) dutiful.

9. *Prosthesis* is a term used to denote (*a*) an artificial part which is added to the human body (*b*) a scientific hypothesis (*c*) the square of the hypotenuse (*d*) a prose theme (*e*) a prophetic pronouncement.

10. A *peninsula* is (*a*) a string of islands (*b*) a string of lakes (*c*) a tongue of land projecting into the water (*d*) a body of water connected to the sea by a narrow passage (*e*) land surrounded by water on all sides.

B. Match each word in column A with its definition in column B.

Column A	*Column B*
1. supercilious	*a.* to stamp out and replace with a substitute
2. superfluous	*b.* more than enough
3. supplant	*c.* predisposition toward something objectionable
4. galaxy	*d.* propensity for something
5. inclination	*e.* romantically chivalrous
6. proclivity	*f.* wickedness
7. iniquity	*g.* haughtily proud
8. quixotic	*h.* brilliant assemblage

C. Using a collegiate dictionary or an unabridged dictionary, look up the etymology and the definition of each of the following words. Then write a brief explanation of how you think each word developed its modern meaning.

1. belligerent
2. boycott
3. coerce
4. collaborate
5. conjugate
6. cursory
7. denigrate
8. metropolis

LESSON 13

cesarian Caesar (*n., adj.*)

A cesarian section is an operation in which the living fetus is taken from the mother by cutting through the walls of the abdomen and uterus. A cesarian section is performed when natural birth is impossible or undesirable. Julius Caesar was said to have been delivered in this manner; consequently this type of operation has been named after him. Caesar, though a family name, came also to mean "emperor or ruler." How did the words *czar* and *kaiser* originate?

imprecate to invoke; pray to (*v.t., v.i.*)

We usually associate prayer with good intentions or requests. One word that denotes prayer offered with evil intentions is *imprecate*, derived from the Latin *in* (to; on) + *precari* (to pray). To imprecate is to pray for evil to come upon someone, or to invoke a curse. Compare the meaning of *imprecation* with that of *anathema*.

manifest seized by the hand (*v.t., adj.*)

From the Latin *manus* (hand) + *festus* (gripped), we derive our word *manifest*, meaning "grasped by the hand." The word has evolved to mean "palpable" or "clearly apparent, either to the sight or to the mind." When some understanding seems suddenly to become manifest, it is as if you were guided to the understanding by someone taking your hand and leading you to the truth.

nebulous cloud; fog (*adj.*)

The Old High German language has made this contribution to English; *nebulous* means "hazy, indistinct, or unclear, especially when referring to the understanding." It is built on the word *nebel*, meaning "fog." The word *nebula* is used to describe groups of stars so far away from earth that they appear to be misty patches, or clouds.

nepotism nephew; grandson (*n.*)

Nepotism is the practice of doling out favors on the basis of blood relationship, especially favoritism shown to relatives in making important appointments. The meaning of *nepotism* is a rational derivation from the Latin *nepos*, meaning "nephew or grandson."

nonpareil no equal (*n.*)

Something of unequalled excellence, a paragon, is designated by the word *nonpareil*, from the French *non* (no) + *pareil* (equal), literally, "having no peer." Actually, *pareil* has its roots buried in the past, for it comes from the Latin *par*, meaning "equal." The word *peer*, as you may recall, also comes from the Latin *par*.

paraplegia to strike at the side (*n.*)

As a result of war, accident, and disease, there are many *paraplegics* in society today. *Paraplegia* is paralysis of the lower half of the body on both sides. *Para* (at the side) + *plessein* (to strike) are the Greek word elements which, when combined, give us the word *paraplegia*.

protean like Proteus (*adj.*)

The influence of Greek mythology on the English language is extensive. Proteus was a sea god who could change his appearance at will; consequently a *protean* person is one who is very changeable, either in appearance or in his principles. Consider also words like *mercurial* (from Mercury); *Junoesque* (from Juno); *titanic* (from the Titans); *iris* (from Iris, goddess of the rainbow). Compose your own list. You will discover that the trade names of many mass-produced products come from Greek mythology. Why is that so?

shibboleth an ear of grain (*n.*)

The Book of Judges in the Old Testament tells of a war between the Gileadites and the Ephraimites. The Hebrews, who were friendly to the Gileadites, could not be distinguished from the Ephraimites in appearance. The Gileadites discovered that the Ephraimites could not pronounce the sound "sh," a sound which the Hebrews could pronounce with no difficulty. The word *shibboleth* (Hebrew for "ear of grain") was used, therefore, as a password to distinguish friend from foe. *Shibboleth* in English means "a test word" or "any phrase, formula, or custom distinctive of a particular faction, party, or nationality."

subsidiary reserve troops (*adj.*, *n.*)

The word *subsidiary* comes from the Latin *subsidiarius*, which in turn comes from *subsidium*, meaning "reserve troops." Today *subsidiary* describes aid or support of secondary importance, such as an auxiliary engine on a sailboat or a supplement to a newspaper. A large corporation might have, in addition to its main office, several subsidiary branches located in major cities. How are the words *subsidy* and *subsidize* related to the idea of "reserve"?

trepidation to hurry with alarm (*n.*)

The word *trepidation*, derived from the Latin *trepidare*, meaning "to hurry with alarm," means "involuntary trembling associated with fear." You may have noticed a dog begin to tremble with fear long before a thunderstorm breaks overhead; or you may feel a trembling in your stomach before going in to take a final exam. In both cases a state of apprehension is present: the dog awaits the storm with trepidation, and the student approaches the exam with trepidation.

EXERCISES

A. Select the word or phrase that best completes the sentence.

1. An *imprecation* is (*a*) a humble prayer (*b*) a suggestion (*c*) an invocation of a curse (*d*) a plea for peace (*e*) an involvement.
2. A *shibboleth* is (*a*) another word for succotash (*b*) a tribal taboo (*c*) a test word for identification (*d*) a worthless article (*e*) a fetish.
3. *Trepidation* means (*a*) nervous agitation (*b*) treachery (*c*) repetition (*d*) cowardice (*e*) effort.
4. To make *manifest* is to (*a*) write a last will and testament (*b*) write a list of military supplies (*c*) make unmistakably clear (*d*) complicate (*e*) make necessary preparations.
5. A *subsidiary* company is (*a*) the parent company (*b*) a foreign office (*c*) a competing firm (*d*) a bankrupt company (*e*) an auxiliary company.
6. A *nebulous* idea is (*a*) hazy (*b*) bellicose (*c*) ambitious (*d*) manifest (*e*) fantastic.
7. *Protean* means (*a*) one-celled (*b*) changeable (*c*) oceanic (*d*) original (*e*) energetic.
8. *Nepotism* means (*a*) practicing black magic (*b*) being a despot (*c*) worshipping ancestors (*d*) doling out favors to relatives (*e*) charging usurious rates.
9. A *cesarian* would be performed on (*a*) a wounded horse (*b*) a pregnant woman (*c*) a Roman emperor (*d*) a person with a toothache (*e*) an orchid.
10. *Paraplegia* is another term for (*a*) a semiprofessional career (*b*) a law clerk (*c*) a part-time job on the side (*d*) paralysis of the lower half of the body (*e*) a plea for hiring the physically handicapped.
11. If something is the *nonpareil* in its field, it (*a*) is a nonentity (*b*) is anathema (*c*) is a typical example (*d*) has no equal (*e*) is the weak point.

B. Match each word in column A with its definition in column B.

Column A	*Column B*
1. coquette	*a.* burdensome
2. bellicose	*b.* serving for pay
3. myriad	*c.* piece of land nearly surrounded by water
4. mercenary	*d.* to request humbly
5. prevaricate	*e.* countless
6. hiatus	*f.* flirtatious woman
7. peninsula	*g.* artificial body part
8. onerous	*h.* pause
9. supplicate	*i.* warlike
10. prosthesis	*j.* to tell a slight lie

C. Using a collegiate dictionary or an unabridged dictionary, look up the etymology and the definition of each of the following words. Then write a brief explanation of how you think each word developed its modern meaning.

1. asphyxia
2. carouse
3. censor
4. courier
5. criterion
6. fascinate
7. July
8. refute
9. sabotage

LESSON 14

abstruse to thrust away (*adj.*)

Derived from the Latin *ab* (away) + *trudere* (to thrust), the word *abstruse* means "difficult to understand." Which do you think does the "thrusting away"—the abstruse subject, or the person who finds the subject abstruse?

alms pity (*n.*)

The Greek word *eleos* means "pity"; from this word comes the Middle English *almesse*, meaning, as *alms* does today, "money, food, or clothes given to the poor." The English word *eleemosynary* is used today almost in its original Greek form *eleēmosynē*, and means just what it meant in Greek, "charitable" or "for charity."

ephemeral lasting one day only (*adj.*)

Derived from the Greek *ephēmeros—epi* (on) + *hēmera* (day)—, the English word *ephemeral* means "short-lived." We do not confine our definition of the word to its literal sense of "lasting one day only," but we do indicate by the word the idea of something lasting a very short time. The word *ephemera* designates the genus of mayflies, insects that live in the adult stage for only a few hours. They are called mayflies because they swarm in May, or dayflies because their lifespan is so short. If you make an association between *dayfly* and *ephemeral*, you will remember that *ephemeral* means "short-lived."

millennium a thousand years (*n.*)

The *millennium* is the thousand years mentioned in the Bible as being a time when good is to be triumphant. There are those who believe that Christ will reign on earth during that period. By extension the word denotes a period of great bliss and joy, good government, freedom from poverty—in short, utopia. The word is derived from the Latin *mille* (thousand) + *annus* (year).

obtrude to thrust in the way (*v.t., v.i.*)

Obtrude, from Latin *ob* + *trudere* (see *abstruse* in this lesson), means "to thrust forward." Often synonymous with *intrude*, *obtrude* means "to force oneself upon others without being asked, or to give one's opinion when it is not wanted."

obtuse to strike upon (*adj.*)

The meaning of the Latin *obtundere*, "to strike upon," is extended in the English word *obtuse* to designate a *result* of "striking upon" something, namely, blunting or dulling the object used for striking. Consequently an *obtuse* person is not very sharp in perception. You may understand easily the meaning of a sentence that an obtuse person would find abstruse. In geometry an obtuse angle is an angle greater than 90°, hence not a sharp angle.

rue sorrow; regret (*n., v.t., v.i.*)

The noun *rue* meaning "regret" is not often seen in modern English prose. On the other hand the noun *rue* designating an aromatic Eurasian plant is in current use. That there is a relationship between the nouns and our more common verb *rue*, meaning "to regret" or "to repent," seems plausible. The oils of rue were used medicinally, possibly the reason that the plant was once also called "herb-of-grace." In the famous mad scene in *Hamlet*, Ophelia uses a double meaning when she distributes flowers and herbs to characters in the play. To Queen Gertrude she says

> . . . There's rue for you, and here's some for me. We may call it herb of grace o' Sundays. O, you must wear your rue with a difference.

Ophelia may have meant that rue for Gertrude symbolized a need to repent, while for Ophelia it symbolized sorrow or regret.

sartorial patcher (*adj.*)

The statement that a person is the epitome of *sartorial* splendor simply means that he has a good "patcher," or tailor. *Sartorial* comes from the Latin *sartor*, meaning "a patcher," and in English refers to hand-crafted apparel.

sibling one's own (*n.*)

Sibling is a word much used today in popular sociology and psychology. Coming from the Old High German *sippa*, meaning "kinship or family" and from the Latin *suus* (one's own), it denotes two or more persons born of the same parents; in other words, brothers and sisters.

sojourn under a day (*n., v.i.*)

A *sojourn* is a temporary stay. It need not be *under a day's time*, but may last several days, weeks, or even months. The word comes to our language via the Late Latin *sub* (under) + *diurnum* (day).

stentorian Stentor (*adj.*)

In Homer's *Iliad*, Stentor is a herald whose voice is as loud as the voices of fifty men. Hence *stentorian* in English means "vocally loud."

striated to furnish with channels (*adj.*)

The word *striated* means "furrowed or grooved." It is derived from the Latin *striare*, meaning "to furnish with channels." A channel is, of course, a groove of sorts; hence the rationale behind the word *striated.*

EXERCISES

A. Select the word or phrase that best completes the sentence.

1. "He is the epitome of *sartorial* perfection" means that he is (*a*) a superb actor (*b*) overdressed (*c*) well tailored (*d*) a connoisseur of wines (*e*) an unequalled wit.

2. "I *rue* the day I met you" means I (*a*) bless the day (*b*) remember the day (*c*) regret the day (*d*) forget the day (*e*) mark the day.

3. *Ephemeral* means (*a*) euphonious (*b*) anemic (*c*) short-lived (*d*) daily (*e*) phenomenal.

4. A *stentorian* voice is (*a*) loud (*b*) hoarse (*c*) affected (*d*) tentative (*e*) mysterious.

5. A *striated* surface is (*a*) grooved with thin lines (*b*) red and white (*c*) laminated (*d*) checked (*e*) decorated with nails.

6. *Siblings* are (*a*) one's peers (*b*) brothers and sisters (*c*) distant cousins (*d*) rivals (*e*) young children.

7. An *abstruse* meaning is (*a*) easy to understand (*b*) difficult to understand (*c*) many-sided (*d*) tacit (*e*) implicit.

8. A giver of *alms* is one who (*a*) gives to charity (*b*) gives to Internal Revenue (*c*) gives to an alumni fund (*d*) gives for selfish reasons (*e*) gives away free samples.

9. The *millennium* is (*a*) the Age of Dinosaurs (*b*) a religious holiday observed once every thousand years (*c*) a distance of a thousand miles (*d*) a thousand-year period of peace (*e*) eternity.

10. To *obtrude* means (*a*) to force oneself upon others without invitation (*b*) to thrust one's head out the window (*c*) to object rudely to the opinion of a superior (*d*) to obstruct justice (*e*) to stand in front of the TV screen.

11. To go for a *sojourn* in the country means (*a*) to make a detour (*b*) to journey by train (*c*) to stay at a reputable inn (*d*) to stay for a short while (*e*) to hunt for antiques.

12. An *obtuse* person has difficulty (*a*) keeping his weight down (*b*) seeing objects at a distance (*c*) understanding fine points (*d*) getting a job done (*e*) controlling his anger.

B. Match each word in column A with its definition in column B.

Column A	*Column B*
1. imprecation	*a.* nervous anxiety
2. trepidation	*b.* favoritism to blood relations
3. protean	*c.* test word
4. nepotism	*d.* hazy; indistinct
5. manifest	*e.* changeable
6. subsidiary	*f.* paralysis of the lower half of the body
7. shibboleth	*g.* curse
8. paraplegia	*h.* incision of the walls of the abdomen and uterus for delivery of offspring
9. nebulous	*i.* auxiliary
10. nonpareil	*j.* to make obvious
11. cesarian	*k.* something unexcelled

C. Using a collegiate dictionary or an unabridged dictionary, look up the etymology and the definition of each of the following words. Then write a brief explanation of how you think each word developed its modern meaning.

1. amateur
2. ballot
3. diurnal
4. hostage
5. molar
6. narcotic
7. nausea
8. sullen
9. toxic
10. vandal

LESSON 15

astronaut star sailor (*n.*)

Astron (star) + *nautēs* (sailor) have both been borrowed from the Greek language to form *astronaut*, a relatively new word. The need for such a word arose when we succeeded in sending men into outer space to cruise in space "ships" among the stars. Notice how many nautical terms are used in respect to exploration in outer space. The Russians coined the word *cosmonaut* for their space pioneers. Why is that word appropriate?

dissipate to throw apart (*v.t.*, *v.i.*)

The Latin word for "to scatter" is *dissipare*, from *dis* (apart) + *sipare* (to throw). One sense of our word *dissipate* is "to scatter, dispel, or disperse." If we scatter something widely, we usually make it disappear. Thus we dissipate our money or time if we are wasteful of it. If we squander good health by indulging in rich foods, late hours, or excessive use of alcohol, we dissipate our health. We most often use the word to mean that a person is dissolute, or has wasted his time and energy to the point of harming himself. *Dissipate* can, however, be used without implying intemperance, meaning simply "to scatter."

esoteric inner (*adj.*)

The Greek word *esōteros*, meaning "inner," is the source of the English word *esoteric*, which means "known only to an initiated group; abstruse." Only the inner circle, so to speak, can fathom the meaning of esoteric music, poetry, or art.

exhume out of the earth (*v.t.*)

The Latin words *ex* (out) + *humus* (earth) mean literally "out of the earth." We use the word *exhume* in two senses: "to disinter, or dig out of the ground," and "to unearth figuratively," as, for example, to exhume an obscure etymology.

exorbitant out of the track (*adj.*)

Ex (out) + *orbita* (track) are the Latin word elements that form the English word *exorbitant*. When you are charged an exorbitant price for services rendered you, the price is "out of the track," or out of the normal range of payments for such services. That which is *exorbitant* is "beyond the limits of custom or propriety."

exoteric outside (*adj.*)

Exoteric is built on the Greek word *exōterikos*, meaning "outside." That which is exoteric does not require the knowledge of a specialist, but can be grasped by the average lay person.

expedite to free one caught by the foot (*v.t.*)

The Latin *expedire* means, literally, "to free one caught by the foot." It is a compound of the Latin word elements *ex* (out) + *pedis* (foot). When we *expedite* the task of filling out income tax forms, we facilitate or make the chore easier in some way. We have "freed our caught foot" and can work in an unimpeded fashion.

macabre dance of death (*adj.*)

Derived from the Middle French *danse de Macabré*, our word *macabre* means "having to do with death." A traditional feature of the morality plays of the Middle Ages was the Danse Macabé, a representation of the slaughter of the Maccabees, which externalized the ghastly aspects of death. Horror and gruesomeness thus become implicit in the word *macabre.*

pneumatic air; wind (*adj.*)

Many English words are built on the Greek *pneuma* (air; spirit). *Pneumatic* means "of or containing wind or gases." A pneumatic drill is activated by compressed air, and pneumatic tires are filled with air. Other *pneuma* words are *pneumonia*, a disease of the lungs, and *pneumatology*, the branch of theology that deals with the doctrine of spirits or spiritual phenomena. We still retain the silent "p" in our spelling of *pneuma* words, perhaps because we can more easily distinguish the written word element *pneu* from *neu*(*tr-*), meaning "neutral," in such words as *neutron*, and from *neu*(*ro-*), an element used in many English words that refer to the nervous system.

sanctimony sacred (*n.*)

Derived from the Latin *sanctus*, meaning "holy," the word *sanctimony* in its sense of "holiness" is now obsolete; the word now denotes an assumed holiness, so that the *sanctimonious* person is a religious hypocrite.

sporadic to sow; scatter (*adj.*)

The Greek word *sporadikos* means "here and there." This word is closely related to the Greek *speirein*, "to sow." The English word *sporadic* thus means "happening from time to time, or scattered in occurrence."

sputnik traveling companion (*n.*)

A Russian word coined as a new name for a man-made satellite, *sputnik* is combined of *so* (with) + *put'* (path), and means, literally, "traveling companion." By the time you have finished Parts I and II of this book, you should be able to create new words of your own.

EXERCISES

A. Select the word or phrase that best completes the sentence.

1. A *pneumatic* tire is (*a*) flat (*b*) flexible (*c*) filled with air (*d*) filled with helium (*e*) made of rubber.
2. An *expediter* is one who (*a*) purchases goods at cost (*b*) deals efficiently with buyers (*c*) accelerates the process of a job (*d*) operates as a middleman (*e*) transports goods.
3. An *exoteric* philosophy is one that (*a*) can be understood only by a special group (*b*) excludes practical concerns (*c*) can be understood only by those outside a special group (*d*) is existentialist (*e*) can be understood by the majority.
4. An *esoteric* vocabulary is one understood (*a*) by anyone (*b*) by a select group (*c*) by men only (*d*) on several levels (*e*) intuitively.
5. *Sporadic* outbreaks of Asian flu (*a*) affect children only (*b*) occur occasionally (*c*) occur in a regular cycle (*d*) reach epidemic proportions (*e*) do not require medical attention.

6. When the police *dissipate* a crowd, they (*a*) scatter it (*b*) arrest it (*c*) call it together (*d*) ignore it (*e*) contain it.
7. An *exorbitant* demand is (*a*) outrageously unreasonable (*b*) noisome (*c*) socially proper (*d*) peculiar (*e*) calculating.
8. To *exhume* means (*a*) to plant a garden (*b*) to inhale smoke (*c*) to plow a field (*d*) to bury a human being (*e*) to dig up.
9. A *macabre* sense of humor dwells on that which is (*a*) absurd (*b*) gruesome (*c*) comical (*d*) dramatic (*e*) insignificant.
10. A *sanctimonious* attitude is one (*a*) sanctioned by the public (*b*) of rebellion (*c*) unquestionably religious (*d*) hypocritically holy (*e*) of materialistic concern.

B. Match each word in column A with its definition in column B.

Column A	*Column B*
1. sartorial	*a.* loud
2. rue	*b.* intrude
3. ephemeral	*c.* relating to a tailor
4. stentorian	*d.* brother or sister
5. striated	*e.* dull
6. abstruse	*f.* striped
7. obtuse	*g.* regret
8. obtrude	*h.* short-lived
9. sojourn	*i.* difficult to understand
10. sibling	*j.* temporary stay

C. Using a collegiate dictionary or an unabridged dictionary, look up the etymology and the definition of each of the following words. Then write a brief explanation of how you think each word developed its modern meaning.

1. centigrade
2. chemistry
3. corrode
4. disseminate
5. exotic
6. Gargantuan
7. juggernaut
8. magazine
9. monopoly
10. sanction

LESSON 16

acumen to sharpen (*n.*)

The Latin *acuere* means "to sharpen." Something sharpened to a point is keen; hence our word *acumen*, which means, logically, "sharp insight" or "keenness of mind."

analogy backward reason (*n.*)

We use the word *analogy* in English so often that we should be certain of its meaning. It is derived from the Greek *ana* (back; backward) + *logos* (word; reason) and denotes a similarity in some respects between things that are otherwise unlike. Analogies explain or illustrate difficult or abstract concepts by comparing them with familiar or graphic concepts. The idea of infinity, for example, is contained in the analogy of an image reflected in mirror after mirror after mirror endlessly.

benedict Benedick (*n.*)

Shakespeare made many contributions to language through his drama and poetry. *Benedick* is a character in *Much Ado About Nothing*. A confirmed bachelor, he is very skillful at maintaining his single state. Eventually, however, he meets a woman more skillful than he, and at the end of the play his state of single blessedness has changed. How this comes about is the quintessence of theatrical comedy. A *benedict* is a recently married man who was thought to be a confirmed bachelor.

culture to cultivate (*n.*)

The Latin *cultus*, meaning "care or cultivation," referred primarily to the cultivation of soil for the growing of crops, hopefully with the effect of improving the product through this cultivation. Our word *culture* is a broadly defined term designating training and refinement of man's mind, emotions, manners, and tastes—in short, all those accomplishments we associate with civilizing influences.

dissident to sit apart (*adj.*)

The word *dissident* comes from the Latin *dis* (apart) + *sedēre* (to sit). When there are dissident votes cast on an issue, they are in opposition to the vote of a particular group. The persons casting the *dissident* votes sit apart from the group, either figuratively or literally.

ebullient to boil (*adj.*)

A person with an *ebullient* personality bubbles over ("boils") with enthusiasm; he is, in other words, effervescent. *Ebullient* is derived from the Latin *e* (out) + *bullire* (to boil).

empirical experience (*adj.*)

The word *empirical* comes from the Greek *en* (in) + *peira* (a trial) and refers to experimental method based solely on observation or on the experience of the senses. The empirical method is based on Aristotle's logic of stating a fact because it seems to be observably true. *Inductive* reasoning is the modern scientific method of working from the facts to a general conclusion, basing the conclusion on planned scientific experiments.

erudite free from rudeness (*adj.*)

The adjective *erudite* means "learned," and applies chiefly to a person who has gained a wide knowledge from reading and studying. The word comes from the Latin *erudire*, a compound of *e* (out of) + *rudis* (rude; untrained). Originally meaning "to take the roughness out of," *erudire* became the verb "to instruct." In a civilization where vast segments of the population were slaves or were untrained except as warriors or laborers, the patrician ruling class held its position because its members had been trained or educated in social and intellectual matters. The belief that the educated person is free from rudeness is based on the premise that through proper instruction man becomes more civilized. Alexander Hamilton held firmly to that belief, advocating that America be governed by the wealthy because they, being the only ones able to get an education, were most fit to govern.

harbinger lodging; inn (*n.*)

A *harbinger* was originally one who was sent ahead to arrange for lodgings at an inn (Old French *herberge*) for an army or a royal party. Today a harbinger no longer runs ahead to herald the coming of travelers, but *harbinger* still means "forerunner." The robin is a harbinger of spring; the thickness of the wooly caterpillar's coat is a harbinger of the winter weather to come; a telegram may be the harbinger of a loved one's arrival. Anything that announces ahead of time is a harbinger.

hieroglyphics sacred carvings (*n.*)

The ancient Egyptian inscriptions found carved on the walls of sepulchers and imprinted on clay tablets are known as *hieroglyphics*. The word is derived from the Greek words *hieros* (sacred) + *glyphein* (to carve). Since practically all of the writing of the times was done by priests, it was thought that the art of writing was sacred.

quintessence fifth essence (*n.*)

The word *quintessence* dates back to the ancient Greek view of the universe. Empedocles held that the universe consisted of four elements—earth, air, fire, and water. Aristotle added to these basic elements a *fifth* (Latin *quinta*) *essence* which he called ether. It was this fifth essence that was the purest and most concentrated, for it made up all of the heavenly bodies. Hence the quintessence of a thing is its purest or most concentrated form. How does Shakespeare apply the word when he has the disillusioned Hamlet say, "What a piece of work is a man! . . . And yet, to me, what is this *quintessence* of dust?"

vacillate to sway (*v.i.*)

A person who *vacillates* is irresolute and indecisive. The Latin *vacillare*, meaning "to sway or waver," provides us with this word, which can denote an unsteady movement or a fluctuation as well as a state of mind.

EXERCISES

A. Select the word or phrase that best completes the sentence.

1. An *erudite* person (*a*) eats with a fork (*b*) is deeply learned (*c*) speaks Arabic languages (*d*) is prone to making errors (*e*) worships the goddess Aphrodite.
2. The *empirical* method relies on (*a*) hypotheses (*b*) observation of facts (*c*) official authority (*d*) scientific rules (*e*) educated guesses.
3. A *dissident* opinion is (*a*) humble (*b*) distracting (*c*) conventional (*d*) disagreeing (*e*) diffident.
4. A person who *vacillates* (*a*) keeps switching from one thing to another (*b*) talks in circles (*c*) attacks someone's character (*d*) increases his speed (*e*) postpones action.
5. A *benedict* is (*a*) a monk (*b*) a newly married man who was thought to be a confirmed bachelor (*c*) a confirmed church member (*d*) a priest who has renounced his vows (*e*) an egg cooked in wine.
6. If you have an *ebullient* nature you (*a*) are a faultfinder (*b*) are enthusiastic (*c*) are easily discouraged (*d*) like crowds (*e*) like to spend money.
7. To be a *harbinger* is to be (*a*) a robin (*b*) a telegram (*c*) a forerunner (*d*) a caterpillar (*e*) a trumpet.
8. *Hieroglyphics* are (*a*) papyrus scrolls (*b*) four-sided stone pillars (*c*) ancient Egyptian writing (*d*) ancient Egyptian tombs (*e*) ancient Egyptian scribes.
9. An *analogy* is (*a*) a collection of selected literary compositions (*b*) a ship's log (*c*) a philosophy of life (*d*) a comparison (*e*) a catalog.
10. The *quintessence* of a subject is its (*a*) opposite (*b*) logical extension (*c*) ambiguity (*d*) history (*e*) purest form.
11. A man of *acumen* has (*a*) a sharp mind (*b*) a sharp tooth (*c*) an accurate aim (*d*) acute appendicitis (*e*) a keen sense of smell.

B. Match each word in column A with its definition in column B.

Column A	*Column B*
1. pneumatic	*a.* to dig up; disinter
2. expedite	*b.* hypocritical holiness
3. exorbitant	*c.* outrageously unreasonable
4. esoteric	*d.* infrequent
5. sporadic	*e.* restricted to a small group
6. sanctimony	*f.* false
7. exhume	*g.* insinuation
8. astronaut	*h.* overly servile
9. spurious	*i.* verbal attack
10. innuendo	*j.* to accelerate a process
11. obsequious	*k.* burdensome
12. polemic	*l.* to attack with words
13. impugn	*m.* relating to air, wind, or gas
14. onerous	*n.* to scatter
15. dissipate	*o.* traveler in interplanetary space

C. Using a collegiate dictionary or an unabridged dictionary, look up the etymology and the definition of each of the following words. Then write a brief explanation of how you think each word developed its modern meaning.

1. antibiotic
2. bedlam
3. clinic
4. gymnasium
5. hermetic
6. jeremiad
7. pernicious
8. psychosomatic
9. puerile

The Second Dimension

Etymologies

Since the English language itself is derived from a combination of other, older languages, it follows that the etymologies of most English words may be traced back to words or word elements in other languages. The *etymons*, or source words and word elements, presented in this section are chiefly Latin and Greek.

We have used the term *etymon* to designate the original word or word element from which a modern English word is derived. Thus, the etymons from which the word *etymology* is derived are the Greek *etymon* (original meaning of a word) + *logos* (knowledge; study). English forms such as the suffix *-ology* we have referred to throughout as *word elements*. Occasionally, when a word is to be completed by the student, we have called the missing part a *word fragment*. In some cases the etymon itself becomes the English word element (*pan; poly*); in other cases the English word element differs slightly from the etymon (*loqui—loquy*, *loquent*, etc.; *caedere—cide*).

Each of the following lessons presents one or more etymons which combine with others to form the basis of many English words. Definitions of words are given only where the meanings of the individual etymons do not suggest the meaning of the word. Accordingly, most of the exercises are designed so that the correct word or definition can be inferred from a knowledge of the etymons.

The word which appears in the exercises is not always in the same grammatical form as the word presented in the lesson. For example, the form *pathology* appears in a lesson, but *pathologist* is tested in the exercises. By the same token, there are cases in the exercises where a number of grammatical forms of the lesson word will all be "correct" answers. The purpose of the exercises is not to test for specific grammatical forms, but to test your recognition of the etymons from which a word is derived.

LESSON 1

pan all

Pan is a word element which has its origin in the ancient Greek language. It has been assimilated by our language and means "all." Listed below are words in which the element *pan* is used. In addition to the main element *pan*, you will note a second word element and its meaning. Usually, when these two elements are combined, the definition of the word in question will be self-evident. When the meaning of a word is not apparent from its etymology, a prefatory explanation will make clear both the meaning of the word and its etymology.

One word in this lesson that needs explication is *panoply*. The Greek elements *pan* + *hopla* (armor) are combined to form this word. Armor is used to afford a protective covering; hence anything which acts as a complete protective covering is a panoply. By extension, a panoply has come to mean any full and imposing array.

Another word whose etymology needs to be explained is *panegyric*. In early days a Greek community often was small enough in size and population to allow all citizens to meet, or assemble. Often at these assemblies a Greek orator would extol the virtues of one of the citizens of the community. The Greek word *agyris*, which means "assembly," when combined with *pan*, makes the word *panegyric*. A panegyric is a laudatory speech or writing.

Last, the word *pandemonium* has an interesting etymology. John Milton's epic poem *Paradise Lost* is the original source of the word *pandemonium*. Satan, a fallen angel, meets with his disciples and makes a formal address to them. Imagine the state of confusion, the chaos, and the din as these countless demons assemble to hear their leader. Milton needed a word to capture the spirit of such a tumultuous occasion. He combined *pan* (all) + *demon* (devil) + *ium* (a place for), and coined the word *pandemonium*, which today relates to a condition where chaos, din, and confusion are rampant.

pan + agyris (assembly)	= panegyric
pan + akeisthai (healing)	= panacea
pan + chrōma (color)	= panchromatic
pan + demon (devil) + ium (place for)	= pandemonium
pan + dēmos (people)	= pandemic
pan + hopla (armor)	= panoply
pan + horama (that which is seen)	= panorama
pan + logos (study of)	= pantology
pan + morphē (form)	= pantomorphic
pan + skopein (to view)	= pantoscopic
pan + sophos (wise; wisdom)	= pansophist
pan + theos (god)	= pantheism

EXERCISES

A. Match each definition in column A with the correct word in column B.

Column A	*Column B*
1. laudatory speech	*a.* pandemic
2. cure-all	*b.* pantology
3. relating to all forms	*c.* pantheism
4. sensitive to the light of all colors	*d.* pandemonium
5. protective covering; array	*e.* panacea
6. one who pretends to be all-wise	*f.* pantomorphic
7. tumult; din; confusion	*g.* pantoscopic
8. doctrine that God is the sum of all natural forces	*h.* panchromatic
9. study of all knowledge	*i.* panoply
10. pertaining to all the people	*j.* pansophist
11. all that lies in a person's field of vision	*k.* panegyric
12. characterizing or pertaining to a wide view	*l.* panorama

B. Complete each sentence by filling in the appropriate word from the following list:

(*Note:* Here and elsewhere in this book, the blank spaces provided for answers are intended as token blanks only, and are not to be filled in by the student. All answers are to be written on a separate sheet of paper.)

pandemic	pandemonium	pantoscopic
pantologist	panacea	panchromatic
pantheism	pantomorphic	panoply
pansophist	panegyric	panoramic

1. ----- is a form of religion that was common among primitive societies.
2. There is no simple formula or ----- for eliminating world tensions.
3. When the party workers learned of their candidate's victory, ----- reigned at political headquarters.
4. The snow, nature's -----, lay on the woodland like a protective white blanket.
5. The poet Shelley wrote a ----- on Keats, lamenting the latter's death.
6. The Greek gods, according to mythology, had ----- powers, in that they could assume the shape of any living thing.
7. Although it is sensitive to the light of all colors, ----- film gives black-and-white pictures.
8. The director advised using a ----- lens in order to capture the full scope of the clashing armies.
9. Without warning, a ----- fever fell upon the town, decimating its people.
10. As I stood atop the mountain, a ----- view lay before me.
11. The ----- is one who pretends to be all-wise, a virtual impossibility in our age of specialization.
12. One might say that Aristotle was a ----- in that he pursued the study of all knowledge then available to him.

C. Write the meaning of each etymon used with *pan*, and then write the English word derived from *pan* + the etymon.

EXAMPLE: pan + logos *study of* = *pantology*

1. pan + chrōma ----- = -----
2. pan + dēmos ----- = -----
3. pan + skopein ----- = -----
4. pan + morphē ----- = -----
5. pan + sophos ----- = -----
6. pan + theos ----- = -----
7. pan + agyris ----- = -----

LESSON 2

loqui to speak

Many English words owe their existence to the Latin *loqui*, meaning "to speak." You will be introduced to a few such words. Study them carefully, noting the meaning of the secondary word element, for this is the key to the meaning of the word.

Two words derived from the same two etymons—*colloquy* and *colloquial*—have developed almost opposite meanings. The noun *colloquy* means "a formal conference," whereas the adjective *colloquial* means "informal in speech, or conforming to ordinary speech."

An *interlocution* is an exchange of words, or conversation.

loqui + acious (abounding in)	= loquacious
circum (around) + loqui	= circumlocution
col (together) + loqui	= colloquy; colloquial
e (out) + loqui	= elocution; eloquent
grandis (grand) + loqui	= grandiloquent
inter (between) + loqui	= interlocution
magnus (great) + loqui	= magniloquent
ob (against) + loqui	= obloquy
solus (alone) + loqui	= soliloquy
somnus (sleep) + loqui	= somniloquent
venter (belly) + loqui	= ventriloquist

EXERCISES

A. Match each definition in column A with the correct word in column B.

Column A	*Column B*
1. talking together; formal conference	*a.* interlocution
2. roundabout expression	*b.* elocution
3. talkative	*c.* loquacious
4. act of speaking to oneself, especially in the drama	*d.* grandiloquent
5. talking in one's sleep	*e.* colloquy
6. using lofty language; pompously eloquent	*f.* somniloquent
7. speaking against; defamatory language	*g.* obloquy
8. art of public speaking	*h.* colloquial
9. exchange of words; conversation	*i.* circumlocution
10. informal in speech	*j.* soliloquy

B. Complete each sentence by filling in the appropriate word from the following list:

loquacious	elocution	colloquy
somniloquent	obloquy	colloquialism
circumlocution	soliloquy	magniloquent

1. Many politicians will not give a direct answer to a question, but rather resort to ----- .
2. The junior senator from Idaho delivered a biting ----- which denounced the proposed bill.
3. The ----- is a dramatic device that enables us to hear a character "think out loud."
4. Ancient Greek orators were masters in the art of -----, or public speaking.

5. A (An) ----- may be appropriate in casual conversation, but it is not acceptable in formal writing or speaking.
6. Many somnambulists, or people who walk in their sleep, are also -----, and say things while sleeping which prove to be embarrassing at the breakfast table.
7. She was the most ----- person I had ever met; one had to pity her husband who had to listen to her incessant chatter.
8. The steel strike brought about a (an) ----- made up of labor and management.
9. A (An) ----- speech contains many lofty expressions.

C. Write the meaning of each etymon used with *loqui* and then write the English word derived from *loqui* + the etymon.

1. venter ----- + loqui = -----
2. magnus ----- + loqui = -----
3. somnus ----- + loqui = -----
4. ob ----- + loqui = -----
5. circum ----- + loqui = -----
6. solus ----- + loqui = -----
7. loqui + acious ----- = -----
8. col ----- + loqui = -----
9. inter ----- + loqui = -----

LESSON 3

pathos disease; feeling

The Greek word *pathos* means "disease" or "feeling." You might legitimately ask, "How do I know whether *pathos* means 'feeling' or 'disease' when analyzing it as a word element?" The answer is, "through association, usage, and context."

Let us examine the one word employing the etymon *pathos* in which the word's definition is not apparent from its etymology. Have you ever attended a movie, seen a stage production, or read a novel which so deeply engrossed you that you felt a part of the proceedings? You felt you were actually living the role or roles of the characters. You shared vicariously in their travail, their joys, and their disappointments. In short, you identified with the characters. With this very strong *feeling* in mind, you are confronted with the dilemma of making it clear to your friend. What word will convey this idea succinctly? The word is *empathy*: *em* (in) + *pathos* (feeling). Remember, an *empathetic* situation is usually evoked as the result of powerful emotional stimuli.

To expedite your work in this lesson, the meaning of *pathos* will be listed in addition to the meaning of the secondary etymon.

a (no) + pathos (feeling)	= apathy
anti (against) + pathos (feeling)	= antipathy
em (in) + pathos (feeling)	= empathy
pathos (disease) + genos (origin)	= pathogenic
pathos (disease) + logos (study of)	= pathology
osteon (bone) + pathos (disease)	= osteopathy
psychē (mind) + pathos (disease)	= psychopath
sym (together) + pathos (feeling)	= sympathy
tēle (afar) + pathos (feeling)	= telepathy

EXERCISES

A. Match each definition in column A with the correct word in column B.

Column A

1. one who treats bone diseases
2. specialist in the causes of disease
3. lack of feeling; indifference
4. one who has a diseased mind or a mental illness
5. sharing another's feeling
6. feeling or communicating at a distance
7. aversion; dislike
8. imaginative transfer of experience
9. relating to the origin of disease

Column B

a. psychopath
b. sympathy
c. telepathy
d. apathy
e. antipathy
f. osteopath
g. empathy
h. pathologist
i. pathogenic

B. Complete each sentence by filling in the appropriate word from the following list:

apathy	telepathy	pathologist	osteopath
sympathy	empathy	psychopath	antipathy

1. There are those who believe that reading a person's thoughts is not possible and hence reject ------.
2. Public indifference or ----- toward voting continues to be a thorny problem in many democracies, including our own.
3. The escape of a dangerous ----- created widespread fear in the community.
4. The politician's ----- toward his opponent's platform was made clear in his inflammatory speech.
5. Osteomyelitis is a bone disease which can be treated by a (an) -----.
6. A (An) ----- is a doctor who determines the nature and cause of disease.

7. ----- and compassion are qualities found in too few people.
8. When a theatergoer feels the emotions of the characters in a play, he is experiencing -----.

C. Write the meaning of each etymon used with *pathos* and then write the English word derived from *pathos* + the etymon.

1. anti ----- + pathos = -----
2. tēle ----- + pathos = -----
3. pathos + logos ----- = -----
4. psychē ----- + pathos = -----
5. osteon ----- + pathos = -----
6. a ----- + pathos = -----
7. pathos + genos ----- = -----

LESSON 4

a; an no; not; without

The Greek prefix *a*, or *an*, conveys the idea of negation. For example, the word *atom* is built on two Greek word elements: *a* (not) + *tom*, from the Greek *temnein*, which means "to cut." Improbable though it may seem, the first "atomic theory" dates back to Greek antiquity and a school of philosophers known as "atomists." These men proposed that there was a particle of matter (which they called *atomos*) that was *not* capable of being further *cut* or divided. Etymologically speaking, the word *atom* is a contradiction and has in our language become an anomaly since the atom has been cut or split.

There are several words in which the element *a* or *an* is used whose meanings are not apparent from their etymologies. You have already met one such word in the previous paragraph—*anomaly*. The derivation of this word is found in the Greek language: *an* (not) + *homalos* (even). But *anomaly* denotes more than "not even." Its meaning is "that which deviates from what would be considered a normal pattern," or "that which is irregular."

Next study the etymology of another such word—*anodyne*. The origin of this word is also found in the Greek language: *an* (no) + *odynē* (pain). An anodyne in a literal sense is a pain reliever, as an aspirin or morphine. The word *anodyne* is most commonly used, however, in its figurative sense. For example, during the depression of the 1930's, when people's spirits were at a low ebb, a popular *anodyne* was coined as a therapy to counteract the aura of despair: "Prosperity is just around the corner." This saying was of course intended to assuage the depressed spirits of a frustrated people. To repeat, *anodyne* is a word which can be used in both a *literal* and a *figurative* context.

Finally, the word *anachronism* needs to be explained since its prefix *ana* does not derive from the negative *an*, meaning "not." *Ana* means "back"; hence an *anachronism* takes you *back* in *time.* As you may have already surmised, the Greek *chronos* means "time." An example of an anachronism is a horse and buggy on a street today. If a teen-ager's parents insist on an early curfew, the teen-ager might think that their attitude toward dating is anachronistic. Since the prefix *ana* found in the word *anachronism* is so often confused with the negative *an*, it is included in this lesson for study.

an + aisthēsis (feeling)	= anesthesia
an + archos (ruler)	= anarchy
a + chrōma (color)	= achromatic
a + gnōstos (known)	= agnostic
an + homalos (even)	= anomaly
an + odynē (pain)	= anodyne
an + onyma (name)	= anonymous
an + osmē (smell)	= anosmia; anosmic
a + pathos (feeling)	= apathy
a + phōnē (sound)	= aphonia; aphonic
a + temnein (to cut)	= atom
a + theos (god)	= atheism
a + trephein (to nourish)	= atrophy
ana + chronos (time)	= anachronism

EXERCISES

A. Supply a word from this lesson to fit each definition.

1. that which deviates from the normal
2. indifference; absence of feeling
3. that which is outdated, or misplaced in time
4. mob rule; absence of government

5. loss of the sense of smell
6. one who does not know, especially with reference to God's existence
7. without color
8. loss of sensation
9. belief that God does not exist
10. loss of voice
11. to die or stop functioning as a result of disuse or lack of nourishment

B. Complete each sentence by filling in the appropriate word from this lesson.

1. Since there were no clocks during the lifetime of Julius Caesar, it is an obvious ----- when Brutus hears a clock strike in Shakespeare's *Julius Caesar.*
2. Temporary ----- caused by a bad head cold can make food almost tasteless.
3. A winter landscape that appears ----- to the inexperienced observer will reveal many colors to the practiced eye.
4. John's disinterest and ----- during the discussion were obvious to all.
5. The dentist felt that drilling the infected tooth without benefit of ----- would be too painful for the patient.
6. Extreme poverty in the midst of great wealth is one of the ----- of American society.
7. After the French Revolution there was an interim period of violence and -----.
8. Concerning matters of religion, he defended an ----- posture, and definitively disavowed the existence of God.
9. "It is always darkest before the dawn" is an example of an ----- .
10. A common symptom of laryngitis is ----- .

C. Write the meaning of each etymon used with *a* or *an* and then write the English word derived from *a* or *an* + the etymon.

1. a + gnōstos ----- = -----
2. an + archos ----- = -----
3. a + chrōma ----- = -----
4. a + onyma ----- = -----
5. a + theos ----- = -----
6. a + phōnē ----- = -----
7. a + pathos ----- = -----

REVIEW EXERCISE: LESSONS 1-4

If the previous lessons have been done faithfully, you should not have to refer to them when doing the following review exercises. If you need occasional help, however, refer to the appropriate lesson.

A. Complete each word by filling in the required word fragment derived from one of the etymons you have studied.

EXAMPLE: an*onymous* = lacking a name

1. -----demic = pertaining to all the people
2. soli----- = monologue; thinking aloud
3. a----- = indifferent; not caring
4. a----- = one who professes ignorance, especially concerning the existence of God
5. -----chronism = something misplaced in order of time
6. -----acious = talkative
7. -----archy = absence of rule or government
8. -----acea = cure-all
9. -----ology = study of the causes of disease
10. -----odyne = pain reliever

B. Write *T* if the sentence is true and *F* if it is false.

1. A *pandemic* disease would be confined to a local area.
2. A *panegyric* is a laudatory speech.
3. *Obloquy* and *panegyric* are opposite in meaning.
4. An *antipathy* is a strong feeling against or a dislike.
5. If you participated in a *colloquy*, you sat in on a discussion or conference.
6. You would visit an *osteopath* if you had a bad chest cold.
7. *Atheism* and *agnosticism* mean the same thing.
8. A word for "voiceless" is *aphonic.*
9. *Circumlocution* is a form of evasive speech.
10. A *panoramic* scene is one that is limited in scope because of an obstructed view.

C. Complete each word by filling in the required word fragment derived from one of the etymons you have studied.

1. pan----- = wide view
2. a----- = without voice
3. -----loquent = talking in one's sleep
4. -----pathy = imaginative projection of experience
5. -----locution = speech between or among people; conversation
6. pan----- = belief that God is in all things
7. pan----- = chaos; confusion; din
8. -----loquial = referring to informal speech
9. -----loquy = defamatory speech
10. pan----- = protective covering; array

LESSON 5

genos kind; race; family; birth; origin

The Greek word *genos* is an important etymon in our language, especially in scientific terms. Depending on the word which is derived from it, *genos* means "birth, kind, race, family, or origin." In the following list, the meanings of both *genos* and the subsidiary etymon will be given. Simply combine them, and you will have a general idea of the definition of the word.

autos (self) + genos (birth)	= autogenous
genos (race) + caedere (to kill)	= genocide
con (with) + genos (birth)	= congenital
eu (well) + genēs (born)	= eugenics
heteros (other) + genos (kind)	= heterogeneous
homos (same) + genos (kind)	= homogeneous
genos (family) + logos (study of)	= genealogy
miscēre (to mix) + genos (race)	= miscegenation
pathos (disease) + genos (origin)	= pathogenic
primus (first) + genitura (birth)	= primogeniture
psychē (mind) + genos (origin)	= psychogenic
genesis (beginning; origin)	
genre (type; style; kind)	

EXERCISES

A. Complete each sentence by filling in the appropriate word from the following list:

psychogenic	genocide	genre
miscegenation	eugenics	genesis
homogeneous	congenital	autogenous
heterogeneous	primogeniture	

1. Hitler practiced ----- in an attempt to exterminate the Jews.
2. Many schools have adopted the policy of grouping students of the same or similar ability into ----- classes.

3. Advocates of ----- classes maintain that students of varying ability benefit from contact with each other.
4. Many physical discomforts or pains are -----, or contrived in the mind.
5. ----- is a word with which a lawyer who is drawing up a will might concern himself.
6. The practice of inbreeding the finest strains of race horses is an example of -----.
7. Plants capable of self-reproduction are classified as -----.
8. The Christian faith had its ----- in the birth of Christ.
9. He was classified as a (an) ----- painter because he limited his work to one particular style of painting.
10. Many ----- defects in children can be corrected if treated in time.

B. Write a brief definition of each of the following words:

1. psychogenic
2. miscegenation
3. genocide
4. heterogeneous
5. homogeneous
6. autogenous
7. primogeniture
8. congenital
9. pathogenic

C. Write the meaning of each of the two etymons and then write the English word derived from them.

EXAMPLE: con *with* + genos *birth* = *congenital*

1. miscēre ----- + genos ----- = -----
2. genos ----- + caedere ----- = -----
3. psychē ----- + genos ----- = -----
4. eu ----- + genos ----- = -----
5. autos ----- + genos ----- = -----
6. pathos ----- + genos ----- = -----
7. heteros ----- + genos ----- = -----
8. homos ----- + genos ----- = -----

LESSON 6

male badly; ill

bene well

Male and *bene* are Latin word elements which you will study as one unit since they are antonyms, or words opposite in meaning. *Male* denotes "ill or badly," while *bene*, on the other hand, means "kindly or well." Several of the words you will study come to English from a language of more recent vintage than Latin, namely, French. These words will be explained, for their etymologies are somewhat inconsistent with their contemporary meanings.

Malingre is such a word from the French, and it means "ill." Its English derivative is the word *malinger*, which means "to feign illness in order to shirk doing one's duty." Should you feign a headache in order not to take an examination for which you are unprepared, you are malingering.

One meaning of the French word *droit* is "right" with reference to direction. *Maladroit* means, literally, "doing things *badly* with the *right* hand" (the superior hand for most people). The maladroit person is not necessarily one who does manual tasks badly with his superior hand, but he is always in some sense "awkward, clumsy, or inept."

The word *malfeasance* reflects the French *faisant*, which means "doing." When an English derivative of this French word was combined with the Latin *male*, the word *malfeasance* was made. The word conveys the idea of "*doing* an *evil deed*." It is most commonly used with reference to an illegal act often associated with official conduct. A public official who has accepted a bribe might be charged with malfeasance in office.

Malapropism is a contribution of both the French language and Richard Sheridan, the English playwright. *Apropos* is from the French, and, as you might already suspect, means "appropriate." Richard Sheridan in his play *The Rivals* created a character who grossly misuses words. Her name is Mrs. Malaprop, and from her name is derived the English word *malapropism*, which means "an inappropriate use of a word."

male + aise (ease)	= malaise
male + apropos (appropriate)	= malapropism
male + dicere (to say)	= malediction
bene + dicere (to say)	= benediction
male + droit (right)	= maladroit
male + facere (to do)	= malefactor
bene + facere (to do)	= benefactor
male + faisant (doing)	= malfeasance
male + gignere (to produce)	= malign; malignant
bene + gignere (to produce)	= benign; benignant
male + volens (wishing)	= malevolent
bene + volens (wishing)	= benevolent
male (evil)	= malice
malingre (ill)	= malinger

EXERCISES

A. The following exercise is a "potpourri" made up of words studied in this lesson.

1. If you slander a person's reputation, you have ----- his character.
   (*a*) malingered (*b*) maligned (*c*) maliced
2. Which of the following would be most likely to utter a benediction?
   (*a*) a witch (*b*) a teacher (*c*) a clergyman
3. A kindly person would probably be of a ----- nature.
   (*a*) benevolent (*b*) malevolent (*c*) maladroit
4. A criminal or one who disobeys a law is a (*a*) malingerer (*b*) malefactor (*c*) malaise.
5. An awkward, clumsy person is maladroit.
   (*a*) true (*b*) false
6. A person who aided you in your hour of need would be your (*a*) benefactor (*b*) malefactor (*c*) benediction.

7. "Pete, I got a bad *disconnection* and can't hear you." The italicized word is an example of a (*a*) malfeasance (*b*) malediction (*c*) malapropism.
8. The patient's anxiety was relieved when he learned that the tumor was (*a*) benign (*b*) benevolent (*c*) maladroit.
9. Cancer is a (*a*) malignant growth (*b*) malevolent growth (*c*) maladroit growth.
10. One who pretends to be ill in order to avoid work is a (*a*) malaise (*b*) malevolent (*c*) malingerer.

B. Supply a word from this lesson to fit each definition.

1. lawbreaker
2. curse
3. blessing
4. humanitarian
5. inept
6. official misconduct
7. wishing evil; of an evil nature
8. word incorrectly used
9. to slander; defame
10. to shirk one's duty by feigning illness

C. Write the meaning of each of the two etymons and then write the English word derived from them.

1. male ----- + dicere ----- = -----
2. male ----- + volens ----- = -----
3. bene ----- + dicere ----- = -----
4. bene ----- + volens ----- = -----
5. male ----- + facere ----- = -----
6. male ----- + gignere ----- = -----
7. bene ----- + facere ----- = -----
8. male ----- + droit ----- = -----
9. bene ----- + gignere ----- = -----

LESSON 7

acious abounding in

The word element *acious* is an English suffix. You will see that words formed by etymons combined with *acious* often denote bold actions. Compare words ending in *acious* with words ending in such suffixes as *ous*, *ic*, and *y*.

contumax (insolent) + acious	= contumacious
loqui (to speak) + acious	= loquacious
mendax (lying) + acious	= mendacious
per (through) + vicax (conquer) + acious	= pervicacious (rebellious)
perspicere (to look through) + acious	= perspicacious
pugnare (to fight) + acious	= pugnacious
rapere (to seize) + acious	= rapacious
verus (true) + acious	= veracious
vivere (to live) + acious	= vivacious
vorare (to devour) + acious	= voracious

EXERCISES

A. Complete each word by filling in the required word fragment derived from one of the etymons you have studied.

1. -----acious = truthful
2. -----acious = talkative
3. -----acious = obstinate
4. -----acious = grasping; covetous
5. -----acious = full of life; bubbling over
6. -----acious = belligerent
7. -----acious = gluttonous; greedy

8. -----acious = insolent; rebelling against authority
9. -----acious = of acute mental discernment
10. -----acious = given to lying

B. Match each word in column A with its definition in column B.

Column A	*Column B*
1. pugnacious	*a.* plundering; grasping; covetous
2. pervicacious	*b.* militant; combative
3. loquacious	*c.* rebellious; insubordinate
4. mendacious	*d.* given to lying or falsehood
5. contumacious	*e.* truthful
6. rapacious	*f.* effervescent; abounding in vitality
7. voracious	
8. perspicacious	*g.* garrulous; talkative
9. vivacious	*h.* obstinate; willful
10. veracious	*i.* clear-sighted; mentally acute
	j. greedy; hungry; gluttonous

C. Write the meaning of each etymon used with *acious* and then write the English word derived from *acious* + the etymon.

1. loqui ----- + acious = -----
2. vivere ----- + acious = -----
3. vorare ----- + acious = -----
4. pugnare ----- + acious = -----
5. verus ----- + acious = -----
6. rapere ----- + acious = -----
7. mendax ----- + acious = -----

LESSON 8

mania madness or craze for

phobos fear, both irrational and persistent

Mania and *phobos* are both Greek words. *Mania* means "a craze or madness to do something." *Phobos*, which has changed to *phobia*, means "an irrational, persistent fear of a particular object or class of objects." These terms have managed to become a part of our everyday language. They are no longer esoteric terms bandied about only by those in the medical professions.

Hydrophobia, in addition to its literal meaning, has a figurative meaning: it is a synonym for *rabies*, a disease communicated usually by the bite of a mad dog.

Remember, each of the following words relates to a mental illness. Thus, though the *pyromaniac* may engage in an unlawful act, he is not a criminal in the legal sense. He is ill and needs medical attention.

dipsa (thirst) + mania	= dipsomania
kleptēs (thief) + mania	= kleptomania
megas (large, important) + mania	= megalomania
pyr (fire) + mania	= pyromania
agora (market place, open space) + phobos	= agoraphobia
akros (highest) + phobos	= acrophobia
claustrum (confined place) + phobos	= claustrophobia
hydōr (water) + phobos	= hydrophobia

EXERCISES

A. Supply the word fragment that completes each word.

1. -----phobia = fear of open spaces
2. -----mania = delusions of self-importance

3. -----mania = compulsion to steal
4. -----mania = addiction to drink
5. -----mania = tendency to start fires
6. -----phobia = fear of enclosed places
7. -----phobia = fear of heights
8. -----phobia = dread of water

B. Complete each word with either "phobia" or "mania" and then match each word in column A with its definition in column B.

Column A	*Column B*
1. pyro-----	*a.* addiction to alcohol
2. claustro-----	*b.* delusions of self-importance
3. dipso-----	*c.* compulsion to steal
4. acro-----	*d.* fear of open places
5. klepto-----	*e.* fear of water
6. agora-----	*f.* fear of heights
7. megalo-----	*g.* fear of confined places
8. hydro-----	*h.* tendency to start fires

C. Match each etymon in column A with its definition in column B.

Column A	*Column B*
1. kleptēs	*a.* confined place
2. pyr	*b.* highest
3. dipsa	*c.* large
4. claustrum	*d.* madness for
5. akros	*e.* thief
6. megas	*f.* market place
7. agora	*g.* fear of
8. phobos	*h.* fire
9. mania	*i.* thirst

REVIEW EXERCISE: LESSONS 1-8

A. Write a brief definition of each of the following source words or word elements:

1. pan
2. acious
3. a; an
4. loqui
5. genos
6. pathos
7. male
8. bene
9. mania
10. phobos

B. Complete each word by filling in the required word fragment derived from one of the etymons you have studied.

1. -----ocide = attempt to destroy an entire racial, political, or religious group
2. -----diction = blessing
3. mal----- = criminal; wrongdoer
4. claustro----- = fear of confined places
5. -----mania = craze to start fires
6. misc----- = interracial marriage
7. loqu----- = talkative
8. -----orama = wide, extensive view
9. -----genic = originating in the mind
10. -----path = one whose mind is diseased or deranged
11. mal----- = inept; clumsy; awkward
12. mal----- = one who shirks his duty by feigning illness
13. vor----- = gluttonous; greedy
14. perspic----- = marked by keen mental discernment
15. a----- = without color

C. Write *T* if the sentence is true and *F* if it is false.

1. A *psychopath* is a doctor who treats mental disorders.
2. A *vivacious* person is often well-liked.

3. Some youngsters see their parents as *anachronisms.*
4. All the members of a *heterogeneous* group would have the same or similar characteristics.
5. A *dipsomaniac* is a person who is addicted to drink.

D. Complete each sentence by filling in the appropriate word from the following list:

rapacious perspicacious
malevolent panoramic
apathetic

1. The ----- Attila wreaked havoc on central Europe.
2. Folk religions hold that we are surrounded by ----- spirits that must be appeased.
3. His ----- reply showed that he had no interest in the plan.
4. His ----- mind anticipated my every move.
5. The ----- view from the mountaintop was awe-inspiring.

LESSON 9

archon rule; power

kratos power

The Greek word elements *archon* (*archy*) and *kratos* (*cracy*) are synonymous. But though these roots have the same meaning, they may not be used interchangeably. *Plutocracy* cannot become *plutarchy*!

Two of the following words need clarification, for their definitions cannot be inferred from their etymologies. One of the words is *hierarchy: hieros* (sacred) + *archon* (rule). At one time in religious history, it was promulgated that there existed among angels a distinct line of command, or an echelon of importance, ranking from the lowliest angel to the supreme angel with concomitant graduations between the two. It is within this religious context that the word *sacred* has become a part of *hierarchy*'s etymology. A hierarchy is any system which ranks constituent parts in an ascending order of importance; thus there is a hierarchy in the church, among living things, in the army, in politics.

The other word is *autocracy*. You might think, judging by its etymology—*autos* (self) + *cracy*—that *autocracy* means "self-rule." Actually it means "rule by one person who has absolute power," and is thus synonymous with "tyranny" or "despotism." The word for "self-rule" is *autonomy* (see page 125). A *monarchy*, or rule by a king, may or may not be autocratic.

an (no) + archy	= anarchy
gynē (woman) + archy	= gynarchy
hieros (sacred) + archy	= hierarchy
monos (one) + archy	= monarchy
oligos (few) + archy	= oligarchy
patēr (father) + archy	= patriarchy
aristos (best) + cracy	= aristocracy
autos (self) + cracy	= autocracy

dēmos (people) + cracy = democracy
ploutos (wealth) + cracy = plutocracy
theos (god) + cracy = theocracy

EXERCISES

A. Match each definition in column A with the correct word from column B.

Column A	*Column B*
1. rule by one person with absolute authority	*a.* oligarchy
2. rule in order of rank	*b.* theocracy
3. rule by the best	*c.* patriarchy
4. rule by the wealthy	*d.* monarchy
5. rule by selected few	*e.* gynarchy
6. rule by ministers of God	*f.* autocracy
7. rule by a male elder	*g.* democracy
8. rule by women	*h.* anarchy
9. government by the people	*i.* plutocracy
10. absence of rule	*j.* hierarchy
11. rule by one; kingship	*k.* aristocracy

B. Supply the word fragment that completes each word.

1. -----archy = rule by women
2. -----cracy = rule by ministers of God
3. -----archy = rule in order of rank
4. -----cracy = rule by the best
5. -----cracy = absolute rule
6. -----archy = rule by a male elder
7. -----archy = rule by royalty
8. -----archy = rule by a selected few
9. -----archy = absence of rule or government
10. -----cracy = rule by the wealthy

C. Match each etymon in column A with its definition in column B.

Column A	*Column B*
1. ploutos	*a.* woman
2. aristos	*b.* wealth
3. patēr	*c.* not; without
4. hieros	*d.* best
5. monos	*e.* father
6. oligos	*f.* self
7. theos	*g.* sacred
8. gynē	*h.* people
9. autos	*i.* one
10. a; an	*j.* few
11. dēmos	*k.* god

LESSON 10

poly many; much

Poly is a Greek word element which is used extensively in English. Listed below are words employing the element *poly*. When you combine the meanings of the etymons, the meanings of most of these words will be obvious.

Polygamy means "a plurality of marriages." The word refers to the practice whereby a man takes more than one wife at a time or a woman takes more than one husband at a time. In *polyandry* a woman takes more than one husband at a time; in *polygyny* a man takes more than one wife at a time.

A *polyglot* has only one tongue, but *speaks* many tongues, or languages.

poly + andros (man)	= polyandry
poly + chrōma (color)	= polychromatic
poly + gamos (marriage)	= polygamy
poly + genos (origin)	= polygenesis
poly + glōtta (tongue)	= polyglot
poly + gōnia (angle)	= polygon
poly + gynē (woman)	= polygyny
poly + morphē (form)	= polymorphic
poly + phōnē (sound)	= polyphony
poly + theos (god)	= polytheism

EXERCISES

A. Complete each sentence by filling in the appropriate word from this lesson.

1. A painter would be likely to know the word ------.
2. A linguist would be familiar with the word ------.

3. A mathematics teacher would have occasion to use the word -----.

4. A student of comparative religion would know the word -----.

B. Write *T* if the sentence is true and *F* if it is false. If the sentence is false, replace the italicized word with the word that makes the sentence true.

1. *Polyphony* is the practice of taking more than one husband or wife at a time.
2. The singing of a barbershop quartet with its multiplicity of harmonious voice parts is a good example of *polytheism.*
3. The ancient Greek gods were said to have *polymorphic* powers.
4. A sultan who kept a harem in his palace would be practicing *polygyny.*
5. A woman who took two or more men as her husbands simultaneously would be practicing *polyandry.*

C. Match each definition in column A with the correct word from column B.

Column A	*Column B*
1. relating to many forms	*a.* polygamy
2. linguist	*b.* polychromatic
3. figure having many angles	*c.* polyphony
4. pertaining to many colors	*d.* polyglot
5. plurality of marriages	*e.* polygenesis
6. plurality of wives	*f.* polygyny
7. plurality of husbands	*g.* polygon
8. voices in musical harmony	*h.* polymorphic
9. belief in many gods	*i.* polyandry
10. plurality of origins	*j.* polytheism

D. Select the correct definition of each etymon.

1. theos: (*a*) tongue (*b*) god (*c*) angle (*d*) word
2. andros: (*a*) woman (*b*) other (*c*) man (*d*) kind

3. chrōma: (*a*) color (*b*) time (*c*) sound (*d*) view
4. gamos: (*a*) form (*b*) marriage (*c*) race (*d*) all
5. glōtta: (*a*) sound (*b*) many (*c*) herd (*d*) tongue
6. gynē: (*a*) woman (*b*) head (*c*) all (*d*) people
7. morphē: (*a*) speak (*b*) shape (*c*) death (*d*) many
8. phōnē: (*a*) fear (*b*) birth (*c*) sound (*d*) shape
9. gōnia: (*a*) angle (*b*) marriage (*c*) all (*d*) god
10. genos: (*a*) wise (*b*) color (*c*) origin (*d*) hatred

LESSON 11

philos love

The Greek word *philos* means "love." Did you know that the word *philosophy* has something to do with love? It does, since it is built on the Greek *philos* (love) + *sophos* (wise) and means, literally, "love of wisdom." Following are a few more examples of words which employ the Greek *philos*, meaning "love." A word of caution with reference to one of these words, *philanderer*: *philos* + *andros* (man). It does not mean "one who loves man." Rather it denotes a *man* who makes *love* to women in a trifling manner—a "love them and leave them" type. If one is accused of *philandering*, it should not be taken as a compliment, for it was not intended to be one.

In the words *hemophiliac*, *philodendron*, and *thermophile*, the root *philos* does not mean "love," but rather "tendency toward" or "attraction to."

philos + andros (man)	= philanderer
philos + anthrōpos (man)	= philanthropic
audire (to hear) + philos	= audiophile
biblion (book) + philos	= bibliophile
philos + dēmos (people)	= philodemic
philos + dendron (tree)	= philodendron
philos + gynē (woman)	= philogynist
haima (blood) + philos	= hemophiliac
philos + logos (word)	= philology
thermē (heat) + philos	= thermophile

Question: How do you suppose the city *Philadelphia* got its name?

EXERCISES

A. Match each word in column A with its definition in column B.

Column A	*Column B*
1. thermophile	*a.* man who makes love triflingly
2. philodemic	*b.* linguist
3. philanderer	*c.* collector of rare books
4. bibliophile	*d.* pertaining to love of the people
5. hemophilia	*e.* one who is attracted to women
6. philodendron	*f.* plant which clings to trees
7. philanthropist	*g.* organism that grows at high temperatures
8. philogynist	*h.* one who loves mankind; one who is generous
9. philologist	*i.* tendency to uncontrollable bleeding

B. Complete each word by filling in the required word fragment derived from one of the etymons you have studied.

1. philo----- = one who is fond of women
2. philo----- = one who loves language; linguist
3. philo----- = plant which clings to trees
4. philo----- = pertaining to love of the people
5. -----phile = organism that grows at high temperatures
6. phil----- = man who makes love triflingly
7. phil----- = one who loves mankind
8. -----phile = lover of books, especially rare editions
9. -----philiac = one who bleeds uncontrollably

C. Select the correct definition of each etymon.

1. anthrōpos: (*a*) rule (*b*) woman (*c*) man (*d*) religion
2. dēmos: (*a*) heat (*b*) mind (*c*) people (*d*) god
3. gynē: (*a*) origin (*b*) form (*c*) marriage (*d*) woman
4. thermē: (*a*) race (*b*) sound (*c*) heat (*d*) book
5. philos: (*a*) hate (*b*) love (*c*) study (*d*) wisdom
6. biblion: (*a*) book (*b*) word (*c*) kind (*d*) feeling
7. dendron: (*a*) wood (*b*) water (*c*) tree (*d*) path
8. logos: (*a*) word (*b*) large (*c*) afar (*d*) measure

LESSON 12

pre before

The prefix *pre*, which comes from the Latin, means "before." It is used in such a countless number of English words that it would be futile to attempt to list them. Also, many of these words are so well-known that it would be unnecessary to study them. You should, however, study a few of these words which may not be part of your vocabulary. For example, do you know how to use the words *predilection*, *precursor*, *presage* (both noun and verb forms), *prelude*, *prerogative*, and *preclude*?

The word *precocious* has an interesting and unlikely etymology. It is built on the Latin *pre* + *coquere* (to cook; ripen; mature). A precocious child's mental development exceeds the norm for his age: his mind has *ripened before* his body. Thus a precocious child may have a mental age of 16 years while chronologically he is only 6 years of age. This word refers to children only; *adults are never precocious!*

Another word which might prove troublesome is *preclude*. It is built on the Latin *pre* + *claudere* (to shut) and means "to impede, prevent, or obstruct." Example: "To *preclude* the possibility of the killer's escaping, the police formed a cordon around the city."

Finally, a *prerogative* is a right or privilege belonging to a person or group.

pre + claudere (to shut) = preclude
pre + coquere (to cook) = precocious
pre + currere (to run) = precursor
pre + diligere (to love) = predilection
pre + fatus (spoken) = preface
pre + judicium (judgment) = prejudice
pre + ludere (to play) = prelude; prelusive
pre + natus (born) = prenatal
pre + rogare (to ask) = prerogative
pre + sagire (to perceive keenly) = presage (noun)

pre + sagire (to perceive keenly) = presage (verb)
pre + sidēre (to sit) = preside

Note: *Presage* is both a noun and a verb. Check your dictionary, since the pronunciation of the verb *presage* differs from that of the noun *presage*.

EXERCISES

A. Write *T* if the sentence is true and *F* if it is false.

1. A *precocious* child is often dull and obtuse.
2. I can have a *predilection* against communism.
3. It is a governor's *prerogative* to commute the death sentence.
4. Thanksgiving is the *precursor* of Christmas in that it marks the start of the Christmas rush.
5. Fortune tellers sometimes *presage* ominous events with disturbing accuracy.
6. A *prelude* to World War II was Hitler's coming to power.
7. A *preface* is a writing found at the end of a book.
8. I am *prejudiced* if I have already formed an opinion before knowing the facts.
9. In order to *preclude* the possibility of an accidental atomic war, the United States and the Soviet Union have established a direct communication between their capitals.

B. Complete each word by filling in the required word fragment derived from one of the etymons you have studied.

1. pre----- = to predict; foretell; prognosticate
2. pre----- = choosing beforehand; preference
3. pre----- = right attached to rank, royalty, or office
4. pre----- = to prevent; make impossible
5. pre----- = forerunner; harbinger; vanguard
6. pre----- = mentally advanced for one's age
7. pre----- = preliminary to the main event
8. pre----- = introductory material preceding a play, novel, etc.

C. Write the meaning of each etymon used with *pre* and then write the English word derived from *pre* + the etymon.

1. pre + currere ----- = -----
2. pre + diligere ----- = -----
3. pre + judicium ----- = -----
4. pre + claudere ----- = -----
5. pre + sidēre ----- = -----
6. pre + natus ----- = -----
7. pre + sagire ----- = -----
8. pre + fatus ----- = -----
9. pre + ludere ----- = -----

REVIEW EXERCISE: LESSONS 1-12

A. Match each etymon in column A with its definition in column B.

Column A	*Column B*
1. pan	*a.* many; much
2. pathos	*b.* rule; power
3. a; an	*c.* love
4. male	*d.* before
5. genos	*e.* to speak
6. archon	*f.* feeling; disease
7. poly	*g.* not; without
8. philos	*h.* badly
9. pre	*i.* all
10. loqui	*j.* kind; birth; race; origin

B. Complete each word by filling in the required word fragment derived from one of the etymons you have studied.

1. pan----- = pertaining to all the people
2. poly----- = marriage to more than one person at a time

3. pugn_ _ _ _ _ = combative; truculent
4. _ _ _ _ _geneous = of different kinds
5. _ _ _ _ _ologist = linguist; one who loves language
6. male_ _ _ _ _ = harmful or evil in nature, intent, or effect
7. _ _ _ _ _locution = talking in circles; evasive speech
8. pyro_ _ _ _ _ = impulse to start fires
9. a_ _ _ _ _ = lack of feeling; indifference
10. pluto_ _ _ _ _ = government by the wealthy
11. ana_ _ _ _ _ = something misplaced in time
12. _ _ _ _ _genic = originating in the mind
13. em_ _ _ _ _ = transfer of one person's feelings to another
14. _ _ _ _ _sage = to predict; foretell
15. pre_ _ _ _ _ = right attached to rank, royalty, or office

C. Write the meaning of each of the two etymons and then write the English word derived from them.

1. pan _ _ _ _ _ + akeisthai _ _ _ _ _ = _ _ _ _ _
2. venter _ _ _ _ _ + loqui _ _ _ _ _ = _ _ _ _ _
3. tēle _ _ _ _ _ + pathos _ _ _ _ _ = _ _ _ _ _
4. an _ _ _ _ _ + onyma _ _ _ _ _ = _ _ _ _ _
5. heteros _ _ _ _ _ + genos _ _ _ _ _ = _ _ _ _ _
6. bene _ _ _ _ _ + volens _ _ _ _ _ = _ _ _ _ _
7. vorare _ _ _ _ _ + acious _ _ _ _ _ = _ _ _ _ _
8. agora _ _ _ _ _ + phobos _ _ _ _ _ = _ _ _ _ _
9. megas _ _ _ _ _ + mania _ _ _ _ _ = _ _ _ _ _
10. oligos _ _ _ _ _ + archon _ _ _ _ _ = _ _ _ _ _
11. aristos _ _ _ _ _ + kratos _ _ _ _ _ = _ _ _ _ _
12. poly _ _ _ _ _ + glōtta _ _ _ _ _ = _ _ _ _ _
13. philos _ _ _ _ _ + dendron _ _ _ _ _ = _ _ _ _ _
14. pre _ _ _ _ _ + coquere _ _ _ _ _ = _ _ _ _ _

LESSON 13

phōnē sound

The Greek word *phōnē*, meaning "sound," is found in a host of English words, some common, others not so common. The more uncommon ones will be omitted since they are for the most part specialized terms belonging to the jargon of technicians and scientists. The following constitutes a partial list of the many words that make use of the Greek *phōnē*, meaning "sound."

a (without) + phōnē	= aphonia; aphonic
eu (well) + phōnē	= euphony
hydōr (water) + phōnē	= hydrophone
kakos (bad) + phōnē	= cacophony
phōnē + logos (study of)	= phonology
megas (great) + phōnē	= megaphone
phōnē + metron (measure)	= phonometer
poly (many) + phōnē	= polyphony
tēle (distant) + phōnē	= telephone
xylon (wood) + phōnē	= xylophone
phōnēma (speech sound)	= phoneme

EXERCISES

A. Complete each word by filling in the required word fragment derived from one of the etymons you have studied.

1. -----phonic = voiceless
2. phon----- = study of the sound system of a language

3. _____phony = harsh, unpleasant sound
4. _____phony = vocal harmony
5. _____phone = device for magnifying sound
6. _____phone = device that transmits and receives sound from afar
7. _____phone = percussion instrument
8. _____phone = instrument for detecting sound underwater
9. phon_____ = instrument that measures sound intensity
10. _____phony = pleasant sound

B. Complete each sentence by filling in the appropriate word from the following list:

phonology	cacophony	aphonia	hydrophone
phonometer	xylophone	euphony	megaphone

1. The _____ achieved by many poems is a result of the poet's painstaking selection and arrangement of words.
2. _____ is a branch of linguistics dealing with the study of sound patterns found in language.
3. The cheerleader's _____ amplified her voice so that it could be heard by the many fans in the bleachers.
4. A (An) _____ was required to complete the physics experiment relating to sound frequency and intensity.
5. _____ can be partially overcome by the use of an artificial voice box.
6. A (An) _____ or some similar sound detecting device is used on all submarines.
7. The _____ of the foghorns wailing in the distance made for an unsymphonic orchestration.
8. A modern version of the _____, the vibraphone, has metal instead of wooden bars.

C. Match each etymon in column A with its definition in column B.

Column A	*Column B*
1. logos	*a.* well
2. metron	*b.* not; without
3. kakos	*c.* water
4. eu	*d.* many
5. a	*e.* study of
6. poly	*f.* wood
7. hydōr	*g.* great
8. phōnē	*h.* measure
9. megas	*i.* sound
10. xylon	*j.* bad

LESSON 14

eu good; well

As you may recall, the Latin *bene* means "good or well." The Greek equivalent of this Latin word is *eu,* also meaning "good or well."

There are several words employing the Greek *eu* whose meanings are not apparent from their etymologies. *Euthenics* is built on the Greek *eu* + *thenein* (from the Sanskrit *āhanas,* meaning "swelling"). *Euthenics* thus means, literally, "a swelling, or growing, in a good way." The dictionary definition of this word is "the science which deals with the development of human well-being by improvement of living conditions." Our governments, local and federal, are certainly engaged in euthenic projects in their attempts to improve living conditions in the cities.

The second word requiring explanation is *euthanasia,* which means, literally, "a good death," from *eu* + *thanatos* (death). More specifically it means "a good death" in that it frees the sufferer from agonizing pain which might accompany an incurable illness or injury. Euthanasia is practiced quite widely in animal husbandry. An example of euthanasia would be the destruction of a horse which has broken a leg. There have been a number of cases in which euthanasia was practiced on human beings suffering from incurable diseases. It is, however, unlawful to practice euthanasia, or "mercy-killing," as it is called, on humans, no matter what humane reasons may have motivated it.

Finally, a *euphemism* is a verbal nicety. For example, when a company fires an employee, we say euphemistically that the employee was "released," or that the company "let him go."

eu + genēs (born)	= eugenics
eu + logos (word)	= eulogy
eu + pepsis (digestion)	= eupepsia
eu + phanai (to speak)	= euphemism

eu + pherein (to bear)	= euphoria (elation; sense of well-being)
eu + phōnē (sound)	= euphony
eu + rhythmos (rhythm; proportion)	= eurythmics (harmonious bodily movement)
eu + thanatos (death)	= euthanasia
eu + thenein (swelling)	= euthenics

EXERCISES

A. Match each word in column A with its definition in column B.

Column A	*Column B*
1. euphony	*a.* mercy killing
2. eupepsia	*b.* feeling of well-being
3. euthenics	*c.* pleasant, harmonious sound
4. euthanasia	*d.* genteelism; verbal nicety
5. euphemism	*e.* speech of praise
6. eurythmics	*f.* inbreeding to develop superior strain
7. eugenics	*g.* good digestion
8. euphoria	*h.* improving the human condition through environmental changes
9. eulogy	*i.* harmonious bodily movements to rhythm

B. Complete each sentence by filling in the appropriate word from the following list:

eulogy	eugenics	euthanasia	euthenics
euphoria	euphony	euphemism	eupepsia

1. The speaker delivered a ----- on the founding fathers.

2. The lilting ----- of the melodic strains drew me to the cafe as though by some mysterious force.

3. Improved breeds of dairy cows have been developed through ------.
4. A horse with a broken leg is sometimes put out of its misery by the practice of ------.
5. Rather than refer to her husband's job as being "janitorial" in nature, she used the ----- "custodial."
6. He awoke in the morning with a feeling of -----; he couldn't remember ever having felt better physically, mentally, or spiritually.
7. The advocate of ----- says, "Don't change man; change his environment."
8. ----- is certainly not a physical or digestive characteristic of one who has stomach ulcers.

C. Select the correct definition of each etymon.

1. phōnē: (*a*) sound (*b*) death (*c*) speak (*d*) bear
2. logos: (*a*) speak (*b*) all (*c*) people (*d*) word
3. genēs: (*a*) swollen (*b*) powerful (*c*) born (*d*) spoken
4. thanatos: (*a*) madness (*b*) disease (*c*) death (*d*) armor
5. phanai: (*a*) to jump (*b*) to mix (*c*) to hear (*d*) to speak

LESSON 15

inter among; between

intra within

intro in; into; within; toward

hyper above; over; beyond

hypo under; less

A prefix is a word element of one or more syllables added to the beginning of a base word which changes or modifies the meaning of the word to which it is affixed. For example, in the word *unscrupulous*, *scrupulous* is the base word and *un* is the negative prefix appended to it. The great number of prefixes in our language precludes our studying all of them. You should, however, pay particular heed to the few prefixes which occur in a host of English words, and whose meanings can unlock the definition of the words in which they appear. In this lesson you will study five important prefixes: *inter*, *intra*, *intro*, *hyper*, and *hypo*. Note: Where the definition of a word is not apparent from its etymology, the definition has been listed in addition to etymological information.

inter + cedere (to pass) = intercede
inter + jacere (to throw or thrust) = interject
inter + ludere (to play) = interlude (an intervening feature)
inter + mittere (to send) = intermission
inter + state = interstate

intra + dermis (skin) = intradermal
intra + murus (wall) = intramural (within one school or organization)
intra + state = intrastate
intra + vena (vein) = intravenously

intro + ducere (to lead)	= introduce
intro + mittere (to send)	= intromit (allow to pass in)
intro + specere (to look)	= introspection (self-examination)
intro + vertere (to turn)	= introvert (one who directs his attention in upon himself)
hyper + acidity	= hyperacidity
hyper + ballein (to throw)	= hyperbole (obvious exaggeration to create a desired effect; often used in poetry)
hyper + critical	= hypercritical
hyper + tension	= hypertension
hyper + trephein (to nourish)	= hypertrophy (excessive development, as a muscle or limb)
hypo + dermis (skin)	= hypodermic
hypo + thyroid	= hypothyroidism
hypo + tithenai (to put)	= hypothesis (assumption; theory)

EXERCISES

A. Complete each word by filling in the required word fragment derived from one of the etymons you have studied.

1. -----bole = obvious exaggeration to create an effect

2. -----vert = one who is not gregarious

3. -----spection = examination of one's own thoughts

4. -----thesis = that which underlies a thesis

5. -----ject = to figuratively thrust between, as a statement in conversation
6. -----cede = to come between, as a mediator between combatants
7. -----mission = something sent between, as a pause between acts of a play
8. -----trophy = excessive development (opposed to atrophy)
9. -----lude = interruptive event, as between acts in a play
10. -----state = within a state
11. -----mural = within the walls (of a school or college)
12. -----venous = within or into the veins

B. For each question below (*a*) select from the list the appropriate prefix, (*b*) write the meaning of the etymon following the prefix, and (*c*) write a word derived from the prefix + the etymon.

inter intra intro
hyper hypo

EXAMPLE: *hypo* + tithenai *to put*= *hypothesis*

1. ----- + ludere ----- = -----
2. ----- + jacere ----- = -----
3. ----- + ducere ----- = -----
4. ----- + murus ----- = -----
5. ----- + ballein ----- = -----
6. ----- + dermis ----- = -----
7. ----- + trephein ----- = -----
8. ----- + specere ----- = -----
9. ----- + cedere ----- = -----
10. ----- + vena ----- = -----

LESSON 16

autos self

Once again the Greek language has made a major contribution to English. *Autos* is a Greek word element which means "self." You should have no difficulty in determining the meanings of the following words. You have already met three of these words in previous exercises: *autocracy*, *autogenous*, and *autogamy*.

autos + bios (life) + graphein (to write)	= autobiography
autos + gamos (marriage)	= autogamy (self-fertilization)
autos + genēs (born)	= autogenous
autos + graphein (to write)	= autograph
autos + kratos (power)	= autocracy; autocrat
autos + matos (acting)	= automaton
autos + nomos (law; rule)	= autonomy; autonomous
autos + nomos (law)	= autonomic (relates to the nervous system)
autos + onyma (name)	= autonym (one's own name; real name)
autos + opsis (sight)	= autopsy
autohypnosis	
autosuggestion	

EXERCISES

A. Match each definition in column A with the correct word from column B.

Column A	*Column B*
1. life story written by the subject	*a.* autonomic
2. dictatorship; government by one	*b.* autobiography
3. self-rule; independence	*c.* autocracy
4. seeing (a dead body) for oneself to determine cause of death	*d.* autogeny
5. self-operating mechanism	*e.* autopsy
6. self-fertilization	*f.* automaton
7. by reflex; acting independently of volition	*g.* autonomy

B. Complete each word by filling in the required word fragment derived from one of the etymons you have studied.

1. auto_ _ _ _ _ = story of one's life (self-written)
2. auto_ _ _ _ _ = self-originating
3. auto_ _ _ _ _ = self-rule
4. auto_ _ _ _ _ = government by one; dictatorship
5. auto_ _ _ _ _ = seeing for oneself (to determine cause of death)
6. auto_ _ _ _ _ = reflex or involuntary
7. auto_ _ _ _ _ = self-operating mechanism

C. Select the correct definition of each etymon.

1. kratos: (*a*) self-acting (*b*) marriage (*c*) rule (*d*) law

2. nomos: (*a*) name (*b*) law (*c*) life (*d*) eye

3. genēs: (*a*) known (*b*) wise (*c*) born (*d*) small

4. opsis: (*a*) measure (*b*) sight (*c*) name (*d*) law

5. bios: (*a*) book (*b*) life (*c*) marriage (*d*) tree

6. gamos: (*a*) marriage (*b*) rule (*c*) life (*d*) many
7. onyma: (*a*) pain (*b*) name (*c*) law (*d*) wealth
8. graphein: (*a*) to put (*b*) to call (*c*) to give (*d*) to write

REVIEW EXERCISE: LESSONS 1-16

The following exercises are a general review of the work that you have done thus far. Remember to let the meanings of the etymons help you to determine the definition of the word. You are studying etymologies, not word lists.

A. In each case (*a*) write a brief definition of the etymon and (*b*) write a word you have studied that is derived from that etymon.

1. intra
2. inter
3. hypo
4. hyper
5. pan
6. genos
7. chrōma
8. circum
9. pathos
10. poly
11. archon
12. mania
13. phobos
14. acious
15. chronos
16. loqui
17. male
18. phōnē
19. gnōstos
20. theos
21. autos
22. dēmos
23. philos
24. gamos
25. eu

B. Write a brief definition of each word.

1. eulogy
2. pandemic
3. aphonic
4. gynarchy
5. euphony
6. philanthropist
7. polygyny
8. polytheism
9. panorama
10. anachronistic
11. anarchy
12. malediction
13. benevolent
14. loquacious
15. heterogeneous
16. interstate
17. intradermal
18. hypercritical
19. hypodermic
20. introvert

C. Match each definition in column A with the correct word from column B.

Column A	*Column B*
1. aversion; strong feeling against	*a.* pandemic
2. cure-all	*b.* pugnacious
3. combative; inclined to fight	*c.* precocious
4. relating to all the people	*d.* preclude
5. interracial marriage	*e.* antipathy
6. wide, extensive view	*f.* veracious
7. criminal; wrongdoer	*g.* panacea
8. irregular	*h.* miscegenation
9. linguist	*i.* panorama
10. mentally advanced for one's age	*j.* malefactor
11. alcoholic	*k.* anachronistic
12. rule by the wealthy	*l.* polyglot
13. truthful	*m.* dipsomaniac
14. prevent	*n.* plutocracy
15. misplaced in time	*o.* anomalous

LESSON 17

circum around; on all sides

counter; contra opposed to or against; opposite

Since the prefixes *circum* and *counter*, or *contra*, are often confused, they will be presented together. First examine the prefix *circum*, from the Latin word meaning "around," or "on all sides."

Three of the following words which employ the prefix *circum* have meanings that are not apparent from their etymologies. *Circumvent* means "to avoid by going around, or skirting," as to circumvent a danger. It implies the use of a stratagem in avoiding the situation being circumvented. *Circumscribe* means "to limit as by drawing a line around." One cannot pass beyond the boundaries of this imaginary line. Thus, for example, if an ambassador's actions are circumscribed by the regulations imposed by his host nation, a kind of circle has been drawn around him beyond whose border he may not pass. Finally, the *circumference* of a circle is the line made by a point that has been "carried around" the circle.

circum + ambulare (to walk) = circumambulate
circum + caedere (to cut) = circumcise
circum + ferre (to carry) = circumference
circum + flectere (to bend) = circumflex
circum + fundere (to pour) = circumfuse
circum + ire (to go) = circuitous
circum + loqui (to speak) = circumlocution
circum + scribere (to write) = circumscribe
circum + specere (to look) = circumspect
circum + venire (to come) = circumvent
circum + volvere (to turn) = circumvolve
circa (meaning "around" in the sense of "approximately")

Next direct your attention to the Latin counterparts *counter* and *contra*, meaning "opposite" or "opposed to." Though these prefixes have the same meaning, they may not be used interchangeably. The list below is composed of words which employ one or the other of these prefixes. Since the meanings of the secondary word elements are obvious, the etymologies will be omitted.

contraband = illegal goods or commerce
contraceptive = preventing impregnation
contradiction = verbal opposition
contradistinction = distinction by contrast
contravene = to oppose, as a law
counteract = to neutralize
counterbalance = to equalize a weight or balance by opposing it with an equal force
counterclaim = claim made in opposition to an existing claim
countermand = to supersede a contrary order
counterpart = part corresponding to another
counterplot = plot that opposes another plot

EXERCISES

A. Complete each word by filling in the required word fragment derived from one of the etymons you have studied.

1. -----plot = to oppose a plot by plotting
2. contra----- = to oppose, as a law
3. -----ceptive = preventing pregnancy
4. -----distinguish = to distinguish by contrast
5. -----mand = to rescind an order or command
6. -----claim = opposing claim
7. -----part = part corresponding to another part
8. circum----- = to avoid
9. circum----- = to limit
10. circum----- = talking in circles; evasive speech

B. Complete each sentence by filling in the appropriate word from the following list:

counterplot	circumlocution	contraceptive
contravene	circumvent	countermand
circumscribe	counteract	contradistinction
	circa	

1. A _ _ _ _ _ by the duly constituted government upset the plans of the rebels.
2. In order to _ _ _ _ _ the danger, the scout had to travel over some very rough terrain.
3. Many politicians are very adept in the art of _ _ _ _ _, or evasive speech.
4. In _ _ _ _ _ to the conservative Democrat, there is the liberal Democrat.
5. The captain could not _ _ _ _ _ the general's orders even though he believed these orders to be in error.
6. The use of _ _ _ _ _ devices is not morally consistent with Catholic doctrine.
7. The serum is effective to _ _ _ _ _ the venom only if administered immediately after the victim has been bitten.
8. Should the senator _ _ _ _ _ the bill, he will lose many votes in the forthcoming election.
9. The club's charter was designed to _ _ _ _ _ the actions of the members.
10. Because the exact date of the historical event was not known, it was dated "_ _ _ _ _ 1746."

C. Complete each word by adding the prefix *counter*, *contra*, or *circum*.

1. _ _ _ _ _locution	**6.** _ _ _ _ _mand
2. _ _ _ _ _ceptive	**7.** _ _ _ _ _vene
3. _ _ _ _ _band	**8.** _ _ _ _ _scribe
4. _ _ _ _ _ference	**9.** _ _ _ _ _vent
5. _ _ _ _ _spect	**10.** _ _ _ _ _distinction

LESSON 18

omnis all

Omnis has found its way into the English language through Latin, and it means "all, everything, or everywhere." The words in the following list have the Latin *omnis* as an etymon.

omnis + facere (to do)	= omnificent; omnific
omnis + farius (kinds; varieties)	= omnifarious
omnis + potens (powerful)	= omnipotent
omnis + praesens (present)	= omnipresent
omnis + sciens (knowing)	= omniscient
omnis + vorare (to devour)	= omnivorous; omnivore
omnibus (for all)	
omnidirectional	

anima life; spirit; mind

Anima is a Latin word which means "life, spirit, or mind." The context and usage will make clear to you which of these meanings is the intended one.

anima (mind) + advertere (to turn to)	= animadversion (unfavorable criticism)
aequus (even) + anima (mind)	= equanimity
in (no) + anima (life)	= inanimate
anima (soul; spirit) + ism (doctrine or belief in)	= animism
magnus (great) + anima (spirit)	= magnanimous
pusillus (weak) + anima (spirit)	= pusillanimous
unus (one) + anima (mind)	= unanimous; unanimity
anima (spirit)	= animosity; animus (ill will)
anima (life)	= animated

EXERCISES

A. Complete each word by filling in the required word fragment derived from one of the etymons you have studied.

1. omni_ _ _ _ _ = everywhere at the same time
2. omni_ _ _ _ _ = eating all (both animal and vegetable substances)
3. omni_ _ _ _ _ = all-creating
4. omni_ _ _ _ _ = for all
5. omni_ _ _ _ _ = of all varieties, kinds, or forms
6. omni_ _ _ _ _ = all-knowing
7. _ _ _ _ _animate = not living
8. anima_ _ _ _ _ = one whose attention is turned toward something else
9. _ _ _ _ _anim_ _ _ _ _ = of one mind; in agreement as a group
10. _ _ _ _ _animous = weak; cowardly
11. _ _ _ _ _animity = evenness of temper; calmness
12. anim_ _ _ _ _ = lively; spirited
13. _ _ _ _ _animous = generous; charitable; noble
14. _ _ _ _ _ = belief that all things are living and possess souls
15. omni_ _ _ _ _ = all-powerful

B. Select the word that best completes the sentence.

1. A lively discussion is (*a*) inanimated (*b*) animated (*c*) magnanimous.
2. A person who evidences charitableness or greatness of soul is (*a*) pusillanimous (*b*) magnanimous (*c*) animadvert.
3. One who is all-powerful is (*a*) omnipotent (*b*) omnibus (*c*) omnivorous.
4. Because man eats all forms of food (meats, leafy vegetables, and just about anything else which is edible), he is classified as (*a*) omnifarious (*b*) omnivorous (*c*) omnific.

5. When many voters are of one mind, a spirit of ----- prevails. (*a*) equanimity (*b*) unanimity (*c*) magnanimity
6. Since God can create or do anything, He is (*a*) omnific (*b*) omnipresent (*c*) omnibus.
7. If you are calm and even-tempered in disposition, yours is a spirit of (*a*) equanimity (*b*) pusillanimity (*c*) animism.
8. The doctrine that all things possess life and a soul is (*a*) inanimism (*b*) animism (*c*) inanimate.
9. A man whose business enterprises are wide and varied would refer to them as (*a*) omnifarious (*b*) omnibus (*c*) omnipresent.
10. A person who has a weak (cowardly) spirit would be characterized as (*a*) magnanimous (*b*) pusillanimous (*c*) inanimate.

C. In each case (*a*) write the meaning of the etymon, (*b*) fill in either *omnis* or *anima*, whichever is appropriate, and (*c*) write a word derived from the etymon + *omnis* or *anima*.

EXAMPLE: *omnis* + praesens *present* = *omnipresent*

1. ----- + potens ----- = -----
2. ----- + vorare ----- = -----
3. ----- + sciens ----- = -----
4. pusillus ----- + ----- = -----
5. unus ----- + ----- = -----
6. aequus ----- + ----- = -----
7. magnus ----- + ----- = -----
8. in ----- + ----- = -----
9. ----- + facere ----- = -----
10. ----- + farius ----- = -----

LESSON 19

caedere to kill

The Latin word *caedere*, after evolving over a period of centuries, has entered the English language as *cide*. Despite the variance in spelling from the original, it still means *to kill*. Whenever the element *cide* appears at the end of a word, the person or thing expressed by the beginning of the word is being killed (*not* killing).

frater (brother) + caedere	= fratricide
genos (race) + caedere	= genocide
homo (man) + caedere	= homicide
mater (mother) + caedere	= matricide
pater (father) + caedere	= patricide
rex (king) + caedere	= regicide
soror (sister) + caedere	= sororicide
sui (self) + caedere	= suicide
uxor (wife) + caedere	= uxoricide
insecticide	

EXERCISES

A. Write *T* if the sentence is true and *F* if it is false. If the sentence is false, replace the italicized word with the word that makes the sentence true.

1. A person who kills his sister commits *fratricide.*
2. In his attempt to rid Germany of Jews, Hitler practiced *genocide.*
3. The killing of a king is referred to as *regicide.*
4. Murdering one's father is an act of *patricide.*
5. Killing one's wife is known as *uxoricide.*
6. Killing another human being is called *homicide.*
7. If a mother commits a murder she is guilty of *matricide.*
8. *Sororicide* is the killing of one's brother.

B. Complete each word by filling in the required word fragment derived from one of the etymons you have studied.

1. -----cide = killing of a king
2. -----cide = killing of oneself
3. -----cide = killing of one's mother
4. -----cide = killing of one's father
5. -----cide = killing of one's sister
6. -----cide = killing of one's brother
7. -----cide = killing of one's wife
8. -----cide = destruction of a racial, political, or religious group
9. -----cide = killing of a fellow human being
10. -----cide = substance that kills bugs

C. Match each etymon in column A with its definition in column B.

Column A	*Column B*
1. sui	*a.* man
2. homo	*b.* kind
3. rex	*c.* brother
4. genos	*d.* sister
5. soror	*e.* father
6. frater	*f.* self
7. mater	*g.* wife
8. pater	*h.* king
9. uxor	*i.* mother

LESSON 20

anthrōpos human being; man

andros man (male)

Anthrōpos is a Greek word that means "human being or man." *Andros* means "man" in the sense of "male." Two of the words included for study in this lesson also appear in previous lessons: *polyandry* can be found in Lesson 10 and *philanderer* in Lesson 11. You may wish to check back to those lessons in order to refresh your memory, since an explanation was made due to etymological inconsistencies or ambiguity.

anthrōpos + centrum (center)	= anthropocentric
anthrōpos + eidēs (resembling)	= anthropoid
anthrōpos + logos (study of)	= anthropology
misos (hatred) + anthrōpos	= misanthrope; misanthropy
anthrōpos + morphē (shape; form)	= anthropomorphic
philos (love) + anthrōpos	= philanthropist; philanthropy
anthrōpos + phobos (dread of)	= anthropophobia
philos (love) + andros (man)	= philanderer
poly (many) + andros (man)	= polyandry; polyandrous

EXERCISES

A. Match each word in column A with its definition in column B.

Column A	*Column B*
1. philanthropist	*a.* ascribing human qualities to nonhuman things
2. anthropocentric	*b.* resembling man
3. polyandry	*c.* regarding man as the center of the universe
4. anthropophobia	*d.* fear of man (fear of people)
5. misanthrope	*e.* study of man
6. philanderer	*f.* man who makes love triflingly
7. anthropology	*g.* one who loves mankind
8. anthropoid	*h.* one who hates mankind
9. anthropomorphic	*i.* practice whereby a woman takes more than one man as her husband at one time

B. Complete each word by filling in the required word fragment derived from one of the etymons you have studied.

1. -----anthropy = love of mankind
2. anthropo----- = fear of people
3. -----anthrope = one who hates mankind
4. anthrop----- = study of man
5. anthropo----- = ascribing human attributes to nonhuman things
6. anthropo----- = regarding man as the center of the universe
7. -----andry = practice whereby a woman takes more than one man as her husband at one time
8. -----anderer = man who makes love triflingly

C. Select the correct definition of each etymon.

1. eidēs: (*a*) loving (*b*) resembling (*c*) abounding in (*d*) human
2. logos: (*a*) study of (*b*) hatred of (*c*) fear of (*d*) love of
3. misos: (*a*) love (*b*) hatred (*c*) form (*d*) many
4. philos: (*a*) book (*b*) love (*c*) man (*d*) father
5. morphē: (*a*) many (*b*) all (*c*) kind (*d*) shape
6. phobos: (*a*) madness (*b*) fear (*c*) love (*d*) study
7. poly: (*a*) many (*b*) opposite (*c*) around (*d*) over

REVIEW EXERCISE: LESSONS 1-20

A. Select the word that best completes the sentence.

1. An ----- animal eats both animal and vegetable food. (*a*) omnifarious (*b*) omnivorous (*c*) omnipotent
2. The slaying of one's father is referred to as (*a*) fratricide (*b*) regicide (*c*) patricide.
3. A man who makes love to women in a trifling way is a (*a*) philanthropist (*b*) philanderer (*c*) bibliophile.
4. The British parliament is the ----- of our congress. (*a*) contradistinction (*b*) counterdistinction (*c*) counterpart
5. The study of man is known as (*a*) anthropophagy (*b*) anthropology (*c*) misanthropy.
6. A philanthropic person is (*a*) niggardly (*b*) a lover of women (*c*) generous.
7. A person who is weak and cowardly is (*a*) inanimate (*b*) magnanimous (*c*) pusillanimous.
8. A synonym for magnanimous is (*a*) philanthropic (*b*) omnivorous (*c*) circumspect.
9. The movement of visitors to Russia today is limited or (*a*) circumvented (*b*) circumvolved (*c*) circumscribed.

10. Should you ----- the rules of your school, you might be expelled.
    (*a*) contravene (*b*) counterpart (*c*) contraband

B. Complete each word by filling in the required word fragment derived from one of the etymons you have studied.

1. circum----- = talking in circles; using evasive speech
2. -----diction = verbal opposition
3. omni----- = all-powerful
4. un----- = of one mind; in complete accord
5. mis----- = one who hates mankind
6. -----cide = destruction of a racial, political, or religious group
7. -----cide = killing one's wife
8. circum----- = to avoid by use of a stratagem
9. -----ology = study of man
10. contra----- = preventing pregnancy

C. Select the word or phrase that best completes the sentence.

1. A ----- disease affects the entire population.
   (*a*) pantoscopic (*b*) panoramic (*c*) pandemic
2. A cacophonous sound is (*a*) unpleasant (*b*) pleasant (*c*) composed of many voices.
3. Marriage between persons of different races is called (*a*) miscegenation (*b*) heterogenation (*c*) homogenization.
4. A loquacious person is (*a*) untruthful (*b*) talkative (*c*) silent.
5. A strong aversion or dislike is an (*a*) empathy (*b*) apathy (*c*) antipathy.
6. If you are hypercritical, you are (*a*) overly critical (*b*) not critical enough (*c*) much criticized.
7. One who shirks his duty by feigning illness is a (*a*) malefactor (*b*) malingerer (*c*) maladroit.

8. A dipsomaniac is addicted to (*a*) drink (*b*) women (*c*) stealing.
9. God, who is everywhere at once, is said to be (*a*) omnipresent (*b*) omnivorous (*c*) omnifarious.
10. One who suffers from a morbid dread or fear of an object or class of objects has a (*a*) mania (*b*) phobia (*c*) pepsia.
11. A dictatorship is an example of an (*a*) autocracy (*b*) oligarchy (*c*) ochlocracy.
12. Should you preclude a thing's happening, you (*a*) aid it (*b*) are indifferent to it (*c*) prevent it.
13. A ----- is a favorable predisposition. (*a*) presage (*b*) precursor (*c*) predilection
14. Referring to a bully as "one who exhibits aggressive physical behavior toward others" is an example of a (*a*) euphoria (*b*) euphemism (*c*) euthanasia.
15. The belief in many gods is known as (*a*) atheism (*b*) monotheism (*c*) polytheism.

D. Match each word in column A with its definition in column B.

Column A	*Column B*
1. panacea	*a.* one who is mentally deranged
2. heterogeneous	*b.* clumsy; inept
3. psychopath	*c.* blessing
4. panegyric	*d.* cure-all
5. soliloquy	*e.* of different kinds
6. apathy	*f.* laudatory speech
7. aphonic	*g.* monologue; thinking aloud
8. malefactor	*h.* indifference; lack of feeling
9. psychogenic	*i.* dating from birth
10. congenital	*j.* voiceless
11. maladroit	*k.* originating in the mind
12. benediction	*l.* wrongdoer

LESSON 21

gregis herd

Gregis is a form of a Greek word meaning "herd." As an etymon of modern English words, *gregis* means more generally "group."

ad (to) + gregis	= aggregate
gregis + arious (relating to)	= gregarious
con (with) + gregis	= congregate
e (out) + gregis	= egregious
se (aside) + gregis	= segregate

Note: The word *egregious* means "standing out from the group" in the sense of "outstandingly bad or wicked."

caput head

Caput is a Latin word which means "head." This etymon is used in both a literal and a figurative sense. For example, to *decapitate* means literally "to sever the *head*." On the other hand, a *captain* is the *head* of a company of men in the army. Try to determine for yourself the meanings of the following words. Where the etymology does not reveal the meaning, either the meaning or an example has been listed for you.

The word *capitulate* has come a long way from its original sense of "to list under titles, or *heads*." To capitulate is to surrender, or give in to demands (perhaps drawn up in a list under separate headings, or *heads*).

cape (as Cape Kennedy)
capital (as a capital offense)
capital (city that serves as the seat of government)
capitate (gathered into a head, as flowers)
capitation (a poll tax imposed on each head)
capitol (building in which a state legislature meets)
capitulate
captain
decapitate
recapitulate

EXERCISES

A. Match each word in column A with its definition in column B.

Column A	*Column B*
1. cape	*a.* to behead
2. captain	*b.* to meet together in a group
3. decapitate	*c.* collection; sum of the parts
4. recapitulate	*d.* head tax
5. congregate	*e.* apart from the herd; flagrantly bad
6. capitol	*f.* social; mixing well in a social situation
7. capital	*g.* to set apart from the herd or group
8. capitation	*h.* one who is the head, or leader
9. aggregate	*i.* to go over the main (head) points
10. segregate	*j.* headland jutting out into the sea
11. egregious	*k.* building which houses a state legislature
12. gregarious	*l.* city that serves as the seat of government

B. Supply a word you have studied to fit each definition.

1. headland jutting out into the sea
2. collection; sum of the parts
3. to set apart from the group
4. to go over the main (head) points
5. outstanding for bad qualities
6. socially active; extroverted
7. to meet together in a group
8. to behead
9. one who is at the head
10. head or poll tax
11. involving execution
12. building in which a state legislature holds sessions

LESSON 22

fidere to trust

The Latin *fidere*, which means "to trust," is used in a host of English words, many of which you probably already know. Since the etymologies of the words listed are not provided, a definition for each word will be given in order to expedite your work.

affidavit	=	sworn statement in writing
confidant	=	one to whom secrets are entrusted
confident	=	characterized by assurance
diffident	=	shy; lacking self-confidence
fidelity	=	quality or state of being faithful
fiduciary	=	depending on public confidence for value
infidel	=	unbeliever with reference to a religion
perfidy	=	treachery; breach of trust

punct; pung point; prick

Punct and its variant *pung* are Latin word elements which mean "to point or prick." *Compunction* means, figuratively, a "pricking of the conscience"; hence if you were to do a thing *without compunction*, you would do it without a sense of guilt or anxiety. Punctilious means "very exact or pointed in detail," as "He was very *punctilious* in his dress." A person could well be punctilious with reference to his speech habits. *Pungent* means "pricking one of the senses," especially the sense of smell; as, "The pungent odor coming from the chemistrv laboratory made my nostrils smart." On the other hand, a pungent remark in conversation is a biting, caustic remark—it pricks the person for whom it was intended. Finally, the word *expunge* means "to prick out, erase, blot out, or efface." For example, one cannot expunge a heinous crime by simply apologizing for it.

compunction = remorse; anxiety
expunge = to blot out
poignant = touching; moving
punctilio = exact observance of convention
punctilious = observing conventions exactly
punctual = on time
punctuate = to provide punctuation marks; emphasize
pungent = sharp; stinging

EXERCISES

A. Match each word in column A with its definition in column B.

Column A	*Column B*
1. affidavit	*a.* holding in trust, as the value of currency
2. perfidy	*b.* state of being faithful
3. infidel	*c.* sworn statement in writing
4. confident	*d.* conforming exactly and in detail
5. confidant	*e.* keen; touching; moving
6. fiduciary	*f.* self-assured
7. fidelity	*g.* act of violating a trust
8. poignant	*h.* to erase or blot out
9. compunction	*i.* one to whom secrets are confided
10. pungent	*j.* one who does not hold the faith
11. expunge	*k.* a sense of guilt
12. punctilious	*l.* acrid; biting; caustic

B. Write *T* if the sentence is true and *F* if it is false.

1. The word *fiduciary* could relate to the Treasury Department of the United States.

2. Having done something without *compunction*, you would feel remorseful.
3. *Pungent* odors are usually pleasing.
4. The president's *confidant* would probably have top secret information relating to our defense system.
5. Judas' betrayal of Christ is recorded in Christian annals as an act of *perfidy*.
6. An *affidavit* is an oral testimony taken under oath.
7. A *poignant* scene is a touching one.
8. An *infidel* is a person who is not to be believed.
9. A *punctilious* person is slovenly in his attire.
10. A person who has *expunged* his feelings of guilt no longer feels guilty.

C. Select the word or phrase that best completes the sentence.

1. An *affidavit* is (*a*) a sworn statement in writing (*b*) a pungent remark (*c*) the act of violating a trust (*d*) a careful observance of duty and obligations.
2. An act of *perfidy* is one which (*a*) is trustful (*b*) violates a trust (*c*) is exacting in detail (*d*) is keen, touching, and sentimental.
3. A *punctilious* person is (*a*) one who does not hold the faith (*b*) one with a sense of guilt (*c*) one who is exacting in detail (*d*) one to whom secrets are confided.
4. A *pungent* remark is (*a*) acrid, biting, and caustic (*b*) not to be believed (*c*) exacting in detail (*d*) one which is sworn to in writing.
5. A *poignant* encounter would probably evoke from you a feeling of (*a*) hatred (*b*) sympathy (*c*) fear (*d*) frustration.
6. An *infidel* is (*a*) a liar (*b*) an unbeliever (*c*) one to whom secrets are confided (*d*) a criminal.

7. The word *fiduciary* relates to (*a*) exactness in personal habits (*b*) a holding in trust, as the value of currency (*c*) a sense of guilt (*d*) a sworn statement in writing.
8. To *expunge* the memory of one's war experiences would require (*a*) remembering them (*b*) blotting them out (*c*) holding to the faith (*d*) an affidavit.
9. Your *confidant* is one whom you (*a*) trust (*b*) do not trust (*c*) have no sympathy for (*d*) regard with compunction.
10. A deed done without *compunction* is done with (*a*) no remorse or guilt (*b*) remorse or guilt (*c*) joy (*d*) poignancy.

LESSON 23

vocare to call

The Latin *vocare* means "to call," and the sense of "calling" is usually apparent in English words derived from it. Two words whose definitions are not apparent from their etymologies are discussed below.

Equivocate comes from the Latin *aequus* (equal) + *vocare.* When a person equivocates, he replies to a question requiring a "yes" or "no" answer with "maybe," or "yes *and* no." The affirmative and the negative are given *equal call.* Hence to equivocate means to give two or more significations to a statement. Politicians are masters in the art of equivocation.

Vociferous means "loud or clamorous." It is built on the etymons *vocis* (genitive of *vox,* "voice," a close relative of *vocare*) + *ferre* (to bear). *Vociferous* denotes a vehemently loud shouting which is deafening. For example, there are those who vociferate against the policies established by our government. Though this vociferating is not deafening in a literal sense, it is intended to be loud enough for all to hear.

ad (to) + vocare	= avocation
aequus (equal) + vocare	= equivocate
con (together) + vocare	= convocation
e (out) + vocare	= evoke
vocis + ferre (to carry)	= vociferous
in (in) + vocare	= invoke
in (not) + re (again) + vocare	= irrevocable
pro (forth) + vocare	= provoke (stir up; arouse, especially to anger)
re (back) + vocare	= revoke

EXERCISES

A. Complete each sentence by filling in the appropriate word from this lesson.

1. The lawyer could ---- no other response from the witness than the invocation of the Fifth Amendment.
2. The judge ordered the witness to answer the questions directly and not to -----.
3. The witness shouted in a (an) ----- manner that he was not attempting to avoid the issue but was merely attempting to protect his rights.
4. This violent outburst only served to ----- the judge, who became utterly exasperated.
5. Again the prosecutor asked for an answer to a question, but the witness's silence was -----.
6. The judge held a closed ----- at which he warned the defense and prosecuting attorneys to control their tempers.
7. As long as the witness could legally ----- the Fifth Amendment, the judge could do little else but ----- the defendant's license.

B. Supply a word from this lesson to fit each definition.

1. in a loud, boisterous manner
2. to incite; stir up
3. hobby; subordinate occupation
4. not capable of being changed or altered
5. to speak ambiguously so as to avoid committing oneself
6. to call back; rescind
7. a group that is called together, as an assembly
8. to call on for aid or protection
9. to call forth; draw a response

C. Write *T* if the sentence is true and *F* if it is false.

1. Were you to be adjudged a reckless driver, your license might be *revoked.*
2. An *irrevocable* decision is one which is unyielding or unalterable.
3. Debating or arguing in a *vociferous* manner is usually not conducive to bringing about a peaceful settlement.
4. It generally is thought not to be judicious to *provoke* those in positions of authority.
5. One's *avocation* usually provides a primary source of income.
6. Many politicians who do not take sides on issues for fear of losing votes tend to answer questions dealing with controversial issues in an *equivocal* manner.
7. A *convocation* of university professors might meet to discuss changes in curriculum and course content.

LESSON 24

psychē mind; soul

As an etymon of an English word, the Greek word *psychē* usually means "mind." In the very few exceptions to this generalization, this Greek word element means "soul." One such exception is *metempsychosis*, which means "transmigration of the soul." In all the words that you study, the root *psychē* will mean "mind."

If you were to try to determine the meaning of *psychedelic* from its etymology, you might come up with "evident to the mind," or "mentally visible." The actual meaning of the word is "inducing visions, hallucinations, and distortions of perception." The word is applied chiefly to the effects of certain drugs that produce hallucinations.

The word *psychic*, although it also has the literal meaning "pertaining to the mind," is commonly used to mean "sensitive to supernatural powers."

psychē + dēlos (visible; manifest; evident)	= psychedelic
psychē + genos (origin)	= psychogenic
psychē + gnōsis (knowledge)	= psychognosis
psychē + graphein (to write)	= psychograph
psychē + iatreia (healing)	= psychiatry
psychē + ic (of or pertaining to)	= psychic
psychē + logos (study of)	= psychology
psychē + osis (abnormal condition)	= psychosis
psychē + pathos (disease)	= psychopath
psychē + sōma (body)	= psychosomatic
psychē + therapeuein (treat medically)	= psychotherapy

psychobiology
psychoneurosis
psychopathology

EXERCISES

A. Match each definition in column A with the correct word in column B.

Column A

1. psychological biography
2. sensitive to supernatural powers
3. originating in the mind
4. treatment of mental illness
5. medical specialty that treats mental disorders
6. one who is mentally ill
7. concerning the interrelationship of mind and body
8. study of the psyche relating to character
9. science which treats of the mind in any of its aspects
10. inducing hallucinations and distortions of perception

Column B

a. psychogenic
b. psychopath
c. psychognosis
d. psychiatry
e. psychotherapy
f. psychosomatic
g. psychograph
h. psychology
i. psychic
j. psychedelic

B. Complete each word by filling in the required word fragment derived from one of the etymons you have studied.

1. psych----- = originating in the mind
2. psych----- = treatment of mental illness
3. psych----- = sensitive to supernatural powers
4. psych----- = medical specialty that treats mental disorders

5. psych_ _ _ _ _ = psychological biography
6. psych_ _ _ _ _ = study of the mind relating to character
7. psych_ _ _ _ _ = one whose mind is deranged
8. psych_ _ _ _ _ = concerning the interrelationship of mind and body
9. psych_ _ _ _ _ = science which treats of the mind in a general fashion

C. Match each etymon in column A with its definition in column B.

Column A	*Column B*
1. dēlos	*a.* knowledge
2. iatreia	*b.* life
3. therapeuein	*c.* study of
4. gnōsis	*d.* visible; manifest
5. graphein	*e.* origin
6. logos	*f.* healing
7. genos	*g.* to write
8. pathos	*h.* treat medically
9. sōma	*i.* disease
10. bios	*j.* body

REVIEW EXERCISE: LESSONS 1-24

A. Write a brief definition of each word.

1. evoke
2. punctilious
3. pungent
4. psychogenic
5. psychograph
6. fiduciary
7. gregarious
8. aggregate
9. convocation
10. invoke
11. expunge
12. vociferous
13. psychiatry
14. psychology
15. decapitate
16. capitation
17. capital (as punishment)
18. psychedelic
19. psychosomatic
20. egregious

B. Complete each sentence by filling in the appropriate word from the following list:

evoke	fiduciary	pungent	psychogenic
vociferous	introverted	euthenic	decapitate
	expunge	invoke	

1. The witness became so abusively ----- that the judge held him in contempt of court.

2. In order to ----- a response from the experimental rat, the researcher gave it a light electric shock.

3. Because its value is based on trust, paper money is a (an) ----- currency.

4. The ----- odor stung not only my eyes, but my nostrils as well.

5. Having found nothing physically wrong with the patient, the doctor diagnosed the illness as being -----, or originating in the mind.

6. A (An) ----- project can be as complex as constructing a new park or as simple as cleaning up a street.

7. An extroverted person is usually thought to be better adjusted socially than a (an) ----- person.

8. There are very few countries which still ----- people for capital crimes.

9. The company spared no cost to ----- the unfavorable image it had acquired in the recent scandal.

10. A witness who fears he may be harmed by his own testimony may ----- the Fifth Amendment.

C. Write (*a*) a definition of the etymon and (*b*) a word derived from the etymon. If the etymon has several meanings, use a word in which the meaning of the etymon is the same as the definition you gave.

1. pan
2. genos
3. acious
4. archon
5. mania
6. phobos
7. kratos
8. male
9. pathos
10. caedere
11. phōnē
12. contra
13. hypo
14. inter
15. intra
16. anthrōpos
17. logos
18. philos
19. dēmos
20. sophos
21. theos
22. poly
23. gamos
24. a; an
25. eu
26. loqui
27. anima
28. bene
29. chronos
30. chrōma

LESSON 25

anti against; opposed to

The prefix *anti* is very common in the English language. There are literally hundreds of words to which *anti* is affixed. But a word of caution is in order. Not all *anti*'s are prefixes which mean "against or opposed to." For example, in the word *antique*, built on the Latin *antiquus*, meaning "ancient," and in the word *anticipate*, the *anti* is actually a variant spelling of the prefix *ante*, which means "before." In most instances it will be obvious to you when the prefix *anti* means something other than "against or opposed to." Where the etymology does not make clear the meaning of a word, the definition has been provided.

Two words may be confused because their etymologies are very much alike. *Antiseptic* means "checking or preventing the growth of microorganisms," or a substance which does so. It is often used to mean "spotlessly clean." *Antibiotic* can be used in the same sense as *antiseptic*, but its common meaning is "a substance produced by one microorganism that acts against another." Antibiotics are widely used in medicine to combat specific diseases.

anti + bios (life)	= antibiotic
anti + didonai (to give)	= antidote
anti + pathos (feeling)	= antipathy (aversion)
anti + phōnē (sound)	= antiphony (alternating responses between two groups, especially of singers)
anti + sēptikos (putrefying)	= antiseptic
anti + tithenai (to set)	= antithesis (opposition)

antichrist (one who denies or opposes Christ)
anticlimactic (proceeding from a significant idea to a trivial or ludicrous idea)
anti-Semite (one who is hostile to or discriminates against Jews)

ante before

The prefixes *anti* and *ante* are very much alike in form, but this is where the similarity ends. *Anti* means "against or opposed to" while *ante* means "before." Hence you should be cautious when analyzing a word which contains either of these prefixes.

ante + bellum (war)	= antebellum (specifically, before the Civil War)
ante + camera (a vault)	= antechamber
ante + cedere (to go)	= antecedent
ante + diluvium (deluge; flood)	= antediluvian (specifically, before the biblical flood, described in Genesis 6:8)
ante + medius (middle) + dies (day)	= antemeridian (A.M.)
ante + mors (death)	= antemortem (compare *postmortem*)
ante + pastus (food; pasture)	= antepast
ante + pendēre (to hang)	= antependium (cloth hanging before an altar or lectern)

antedate
anterior
anticipate
antique

EXERCISES

A. Match each word in column A with its definition in column B.

Column A	*Column B*
1. antependium	*a.* before the biblical flood; hence, antiquated
2. antemeridian	*b.* outer chamber; waiting room
3. antidote	*c.* cloth hanging before an altar or pulpit
4. antecedent	*d.* going before in time or place
5. antiseptic	*e.* before the war (especially the Civil War)
6. antithesis	*f.* appetizer
7. antediluvian	*g.* before noon
8. antepast	*h.* remedy given to counteract effects of poison
9. antibiotic	*i.* substance which checks the growth of microorganisms
10. antechamber	*j.* substance produced by one microorganism that acts against another
11. antipathy	*k.* strong aversion or dislike
12. antebellum	*l.* opposition or contrast of ideas

B. Complete each word by filling in the required word fragment derived from one of the etymons you have studied.

1. ante_ _ _ _ _ = before the biblical flood; antiquated
2. anti_ _ _ _ _ = remedy to counteract the effects of poison
3. ante_ _ _ _ _ = cloth hanging in front of an altar or pulpit
4. ante_ _ _ _ _ = waiting room
5. ante_ _ _ _ _ = going before in time or place
6. ante_ _ _ _ _ = before the war (especially the Civil War)

7. anti_ _ _ _ _ = substance checking growth of microscopic organisms
8. ante_ _ _ _ _ = appetizer
9. ante_ _ _ _ _ = before noon
10. anti_ _ _ _ _ = opposition or contrast of ideas
11. anti_ _ _ _ _ = strong aversion or dislike
12. anti_ _ _ _ _ = substance produced by one microorganism that opposes the action of another

C. Write the meaning of each etymon used with *anti* or *ante* and then write the English word derived from *anti* or *ante* + the etymon.

1. anti + tithenai _ _ _ _ _ = _ _ _ _ _
2. anti + pathos _ _ _ _ _ = _ _ _ _ _
3. anti + bios _ _ _ _ _ = _ _ _ _ _
4. anti + sēptikos _ _ _ _ _ = _ _ _ _ _
5. ante + medius _ _ _ _ _ + dies _ _ _ _ _ = _ _ _ _ _
6. ante + bellum _ _ _ _ _ = _ _ _ _ _
7. ante + cedere _ _ _ _ _ = _ _ _ _ _
8. ante + diluvium _ _ _ _ _ = _ _ _ _ _
9. ante + mors _ _ _ _ _ = _ _ _ _ _
10. ante + pastus _ _ _ _ _ = _ _ _ _ _

LESSON 26

retro back; behind

The prefix *retro* is a Latin word element which means "back or behind." Note that in the subsequent list *retrospect* does not mean a "looking back" as over the shoulder; rather, it denotes a looking back on past events or a reflecting on such happenings. For example: "When he viewed his childhood in retrospect, he could understand his bitterness toward school."

retro + agere (to drive) = retroactive (effective as of a prior date)
retro + cedere (to go) = retrocede
retro + flectere (to bend) = retroflex
retro + gradi (to go) = retrogression
retro + lingua (tongue) = retrolingual
retro + specere (to look) = retrospect
retro + vertere (to turn) = retroversion
retro-rocket

pro before; forward

While *retro* means "back or behind," the prefix *pro* means "forward or before." These prefixes are opposite in meaning. In some instances information in addition to the etymologies of words will be provided to expedite your work.

pro + crastinus (of tomorrow) = procrastinate (delay; postpone)
pro + gignere (to beget) = progenitor (ancestor); progeny (offspring)
pro + gnōsis (knowledge) = prognosis
pro + gradi (to go) = progress
pro + liquēre (to be fluid) = prolix (unduly prolonged)

pro + logos (word)	= prologue
pro + miscēre (to mix)	= promiscuous (indiscriminately distributed)
pro + phanai (to speak)	= prophet
pro + phylassein (to guard)	= prophylactic
pro + ponere (to put)	= propound
pro + specere (to look)	= prospect
pro + sternere (to throw down)	= prostrate (quite different from the *prostate* gland)

EXERCISES

A. Complete each word by filling in the required word fragment derived from one of the etymons you have studied.

1. pro----- = a look forward
2. pro----- = to put off from day to day; delay
3. pro----- = lying flat on the ground
4. pro----- = to propose; offer for consideration
5. pro----- = forefather
6. pro----- = introduction to a discourse, poem, etc.
7. pro----- = forecast; prediction
8. pro----- = to go forward
9. retro----- = act or process of turning back
10. retro----- = a look back on things past
11. retro----- = to recede; go back
12. retro----- = a stepping or moving backward
13. retro----- = bent back, as the tongue in pronouncing certain sounds in English
14. retro----- = effective as of a given date in the past

B. Complete each sentence by filling in the appropriate word from this lesson.

1. On the basis of an exhaustive examination, the doctor made a ----- which indicated complete recovery within a year.
2. One can discover many mistakes and follies made in life when viewing it in -----.
3. Many opportunities are lost forever simply because we ----- and do not act quickly enough.
4. In the author's -----, he stated his purpose in writing the novel.
5. The ----- in her child's reading ability was ascribed by the mother to poor teaching.
6. The salary increase given in March was made ----- to the preceding January.
7. In many primitive religious cults, it was mandatory that adherents ----- themselves before their pagan gods.
8. John was about to ----- an alternate proposal when he was declared out of order by the chairman.
9. The tongue must ----- in order to pronounce many sounds made in English.

C. Select the correct definition of each etymon.

1. vertere: (*a*) to see (*b*) to turn (*c*) to look (*d*) to step
2. cedere: (*a*) to turn (*b*) to take (*c*) to go (*d*) to look
3. gnōsis: (*a*) knowledge (*b*) belief (*c*) writing (*d*) truth
4. logos: (*a*) tongue (*b*) sacred (*c*) word (*d*) healing
5. miscēre: (*a*) to put (*b*) to mix (*c*) to beget (*d*) to step
6. specere: (*a*) to look (*b*) to hang (*c*) to speak (*d*) to put
7. flectere: (*a*) to bend (*b*) to step (*c*) to go (*d*) to drink
8. phylassein: (*a*) to collect (*b*) to guard (*c*) to put (*d*) to throw
9. phanai: (*a*) to fear (*b*) to turn (*c*) to send (*d*) to speak
10. ponere: (*a*) to put (*b*) to pound (*c*) to know (*d*) to quarrel

LESSON 27

logos study or science of; word or speech

Countless words in English employ the Greek etymon *logos*. The English version of *logos* is *ology*. This Greek word element has two different meanings: "study or science of" and "word or speech." Usually the meaning of *logos* will be "study or science of." If not otherwise designated, the meaning of *ology* in the following words will be "study or science of."

anthrōpos (man) + logos	= anthropology
chronos (time) + logos	= chronology
ethnos (nation) + logos	= ethnology
etymos (true) + logos (word)	= etymology
ichthys (fish) + logos	= ichthyology
kosmos (world) + logos	= cosmology
morphē (form) + logos	= morphology (study of structural organic types; branch of linguistics)
nekros (dead body) + logos	= necrology (an obituary notice)
ornis (bird) + logos	= ornithology
palaios (ancient) + logos	= paleontology (study of fossils)
petra (rock) + logos	= petrology
philos (love) + logos (word)	= philology (study of languages)
phōnē (sound) + logos	= phonology
pseudēs (false) + logos	= pseudology (false science)
tauto (same) + logos (word)	= tautology (redundancy; needless repetition)

EXERCISES

A. Write *T* if the sentence is true and *F* if it is false.

1. *Petrology* is a branch of geology.
2. *Ornithology* is the study of rocks.
3. *Ichthyology* is indirectly concerned with the ocean.
4. A *paleontologist* would be vitally concerned with the discovery of an ancient Egyptian crypt or tomb.
5. A historian would be very much interested in a *chronology* of important events.
6. A philosopher might well study questions of a *cosmological* nature.
7. An *ethnologist* would probably study the mores of cultures.
8. A dictionary writer (lexicographer) makes use of *etymological* data in his work.
9. A *necrology* is referred to as an obituary.
10. A *tautological* expression is in some way repetitious.
11. A linguist in his study of language is intimately concerned with its *phonological* values.
12. A *philologist* concerns himself with the growth and development of language.

B. Write the meaning of each etymon used with *logos* and then write the English word derived from *logos* + the etymon.

1. philos ----- + logos = -----
2. phōnē ----- + logos = -----
3. petra ----- + logos = -----
4. etymos ----- + logos = -----
5. ornis ----- + logos = -----
6. ichthys ----- + logos = -----
7. palaios ----- + logos = -----
8. morphē ----- + logos = -----
9. anthrōpos ----- + logos = -----
10. chronos ----- + logos = -----

REVIEW EXERCISE: LESSONS 1-27

A. Complete each word by filling in the required word fragment derived from one of the etymons you have studied.

1. -----spect = a look back in time
2. retro----- = to go or move backward
3. phon----- = sound system of a language
4. -----ologist = one who loves language; linguist
5. -----meridian = before noon (A.M.)
6. anti----- = strong feeling against; aversion
7. ante----- = going before in place or time
8. pro----- = to hesitate; delay; postpone
9. -----genitor = forefather; ancestor
10. pro----- = to know in advance; predict
11. -----logue = preface
12. -----ology = science or study of man

B. Select the word or phrase that best completes the sentence.

1. A child who is mentally advanced is said to be (*a*) prodigious (*b*) precocious (*c*) precluded.
2. A speech made by an actor alone on the stage is a (*a*) moniloquy (*b*) monogram (*c*) soliloquy.
3. A person who equivocates is guilty of (*a*) lying (*b*) boasting (*c*) talking too much.
4. A panoramic scene is one which affords a (*a*) wide view (*b*) pretty view (*c*) restricted view.
5. Gregarious means (*a*) sheepish (*b*) sociable (*c*) sly.
6. To behead means to (*a*) decapitate (*b*) capitulate (*c*) capitate.
7. A predilection is a (*a*) dislike (*b*) preference (*c*) prediction.
8. Vociferous means (*a*) vocally loud (*b*) greedy (*c*) abundant.
9. An autocracy is a form of (*a*) kingship (*b*) dictatorship (*c*) democracy.

10. Pathology is the study or science of (*a*) feelings (*b*) disease (*c*) topography.
11. The doctrine that God does not exist is (*a*) agnosticism (*b*) polytheism (*c*) atheism.
12. An anachronism is something which is not in keeping with the (*a*) time (*b*) decor (*c*) environment.
13. The mass killing of members of a particular racial, political, or religious group is known as (*a*) regicide (*b*) uxoricide (*c*) genocide.
14. A malediction is a (*a*) blessing (*b*) curse (*c*) solecism.
15. A clumsy person is characterized as being (*a*) malevolent (*b*) maleficent (*c*) maladroit.
16. A loquacious person is (*a*) belligerent (*b*) obstinate (*c*) talkative.
17. A dread fear of an object or class of objects is a (*a*) mania (*b*) phobia (*c*) psychogenesis.
18. To preclude means to (*a*) prevent (*b*) aid (*c*) know beforehand.
19. Aphonic means (*a*) noisy (*b*) voiceless (*c*) colorless.
20. To avoid a situation is to (*a*) circumscribe it (*b*) circumvent it (*c*) circumvolve it.

C. Write (*a*) a definition of the etymon and (*b*) a word derived from the etymon. If the etymon has several meanings, use a word in which the meaning of the etymon is the same as the definition you gave.

1. pan
2. counter
3. circum
4. inter
5. intra
6. gnōsis
7. genos
8. a; an
9. poly
10. theos
11. male
12. pathos
13. retro
14. ante
15. anti
16. bios
17. vertere
18. logos
19. chrōma
20. chronos

D. Write *T* if the sentence is true and *F* if it is false.

1. An *anodyne* is an assumed name.
2. A *polyglot* is a linguist, or one who speaks several languages.
3. *Anthropology* is the study of man.
4. A *pungent* odor is sharp or biting.
5. A *punctilious* person is usually slovenly in appearance.
6. The Pentagon is more concerned with *fiduciary* matters than is the Treasury Department.
7. A *psychogenic* illness is one which originates in the mind.
8. To *equivocate* is to speak loudly.
9. Should you commit an act without *compunction*, it is an action taken without regret.
10. A *misanthrope* hates mankind.
11. The words *philanthropist* and *misanthrope* are opposite in meaning.
12. To *circumscribe* means to limit.
13. *Autonomy* means self-rule or independence.
14. *Hypercritical* means excessively critical.

LESSON 28

verus true

vertere to turn

Since the Latin words *verus* and *vertere* are so similar in sound and appearance, they will be presented together. You can then note similarities and differences between them. *Vertere* signifies "to turn," and *verus* means "true." Very often the context in which the word appears will afford you sufficient information to determine which of the etymons it is derived from. Where the meaning of a word in the following list is not obvious, a brief definition is given.

Subvert and *pervert* are sometimes used synonymously: for example, that which subverts a person's morals also perverts them. The two words do, however, have distinct meanings. To subvert is to undermine, to ruin, to destroy by eating away at the foundation. To pervert is to turn aside from that which is good or true, to twist, to corrupt.

con (with) + vertere	= convert; conversion
contra (against) + vertere	= controvert
extro (outward) + vertere	= extrovert (one whose interests are turned outside himself)
in (not) + ad (to) + vertere	= inadvertent (heedless; accidental)
in (in) + vertere	= invert; inversion
intro (within) + vertere	= introvert (opposite of extrovert)
per (thoroughly) + vertere	= pervert; perversion
sub (under) + vertere	= subvert; subversion
convertible	
vertigo (dizziness)	

verus (true) + acious (abounding in) = veracious; veracity
verus (true) + dictum (saying) = verdict (decision of the jury in a trial)
verus (true) + similis (similar) = verisimilitude
veracity (conformity with truth or fact)
verify
verily
veritable
verity (true fact or statement)

EXERCISES

A. Complete each word by filling in the required word fragment(s) derived from the etymons you have studied.

1. -----vert----- = not paying attention; unintentional
2. ver----- = truthful
3. -----vers----- = reversal of position, order, or relationship
4. -----vert = to oppose or turn against
5. -----vert = one turned within himself
6. ver----- = similarity to the truth
7. vert----- = dizziness
8. -----vert = one turned outward; gregarious person
9. -----vert = to undermine
10. -----vert = to cause to turn away from the true course

B. Complete each sentence by filling in the appropriate word from this lesson.

1. He was a ----- from Christianity to Judaism.
2. Some people suffer from ----- when they look down from a great height.

3. Mr. Smith taught his children to be ----- in all matters, even when telling the truth was painful.
4. The primary objective of a revolutionary party is the ------ of the government.
5. It is often better to tell an outright lie than to ----- the truth.
6. The artist had achieved such great ----- in his picture that the painted fruit looked like real fruit.
7. Making an impatient gesture, the instructor ----- let his pen drop to the floor.
8. In order to ----- the testimony of the witness, the lawyer called in a leading psychiatrist.
9. He was a (an) ----- Romeo when it came to women.
10. The ----- of his testimony could easily be checked by the police.

C. Write the meaning of each etymon used with *vertere* or *verus* and then write the English word derived from *vertere* or *verus* + the etymon.

1. extro ----- + vertere = -----
2. intro ----- + vertere = -----
3. per ----- + vertere = -----
4. con ----- + vertere = -----
5. contra ----- + vertere = -----
6. sub ----- + vertere = -----
7. verus + acious ----- = -----
8. verus + similis ----- = -----
9. in ----- + ad ----- + vertere = -----

LESSON 29

ob against; in the way of

The Latin prefix *ob*, which often changes to *o*, *oc*, or *op*, means "against" or "in the way of." It is not necessary to delve into the linguistics which underlie the reasons for the variations in spelling. Simply remember that there are several forms of the prefix *ob*.

You should have little difficulty with the subsequent exercise, for the meaning of each etymon should give you sufficient information for a loose definition of the word. Where the etymology of a word is not clear or is doubtful, a very general definition will be given.

ob (against) + claudere (to shut) = occlude (block)

ob (against) + durare (to last) = obdurate (stubborn; unyielding)

ob (against) + edere (to eat) = obese (fat; overweight)

ob (against) + loqui (to speak) = obloquy (condemnation)

ob (in the way of) + noxa (harm) = obnoxious (offensive)

ob (against) + premere (to press) = oppress

ob (in the way of) + probrum (reproach) = opprobrium; opprobrious

ob (against) + pugnare (to fight) = oppugn (call in question; attack) ob (against) + strepere (to make a noise) = obstreperous (unruly; noisy)

ob (against) + trudere (to thrust) = obtrude (intrude)

EXERCISES

A. Match each definition in column A with the correct word from column B.

Column A	*Column B*
1. to shut off; cut off; obstruct	*a.* opprobrium
2. very fat	*b.* oppress
3. noisy and unruly	*c.* occlude
4. verbal attack; condemnation	*d.* obese
5. offensive; bothersome	*e.* obtrude
6. inflexible; intractable	*f.* obstreperous
7. to intrude	*g.* oppugn
8. reproach; disgrace that follows bad conduct	*h.* obloquy
	i. obnoxious
9. to crush; trample	*j.* obdurate
10. to assail; call into question	

B. Complete each sentence by filling in the appropriate word from this lesson.

1. The doctor explained to his patient that should a coronary artery -----, the consequences could be fatal.

2. We desperately avoid the braggart who constantly ----- himself upon us, bringing with him tales of personal derring-do.

3. The young student was ----- in his refusal to comply with school regulations; neither reason nor force could move him.

4. He shuddered to contemplate the prolonged visit of his ----- young nephew, who was sure to intrude upon the quiet of his home.
5. The salesman's technique was so ----- that he was forcibly ejected from many homes.
6. In order to strengthen his case, the lawyer attempted to ----- the character of the state's prime witness.
7. An autocratic ruler knows well that he must first win over the military before he can ----- a people.
8. My ----- friend found it most trying to adhere to the diet prescribed by his doctor while I was partaking of a delicious banana split.
9. The ----- that accompanies a prison sentence often makes it difficult for an ex-convict to find gainful employment.
10. The principal delivered a scathing ----- to the assembly of students for their opprobrious conduct at the game.

C. Select the correct definition of each etymon.

1. premere: (*a*) to begin (*b*) to press (*c*) to see (*d*) to precede
2. probrum: (*a*) judgment (*b*) fear (*c*) reproach (*d*) fat
3. noxa: (*a*) harm (*b*) hard (*c*) plant (*d*) wall
4. loqui: (*a*) to write (*b*) to shut (*c*) to speak (*d*) to fight
5. strepere: (*a*) to make a noise (*b*) to plough (*c*) to follow (*d*) to believe
6. trudere: (*a*) to harden (*b*) to pull (*c*) to testify (*d*) to thrust
7. durare: (*a*) to last (*b*) to grow (*c*) to make a noise (*d*) to enter
8. edere: (*a*) to avoid (*b*) to fly (*c*) to eat (*d*) to turn to
9. claudere: (*a*) to clap (*b*) to bend (*c*) to mold (*d*) to shut
10. pugnare: (*a*) to fight (*b*) to reproach (*c*) to lie (*d*) to push

LESSON 30

Terms which deal with the medical or paramedical professions occur more and more frequently in general reading and conversation. You should therefore acquaint yourself with a few such specialized words. A brief prefatory statement about three of the words to be presented may prove helpful.

First study the etymology of the word *orthopedist.* It is built on the Greek words *orthos* (straight; correct) + *paidos* (child). The latter etymon is the troublesome one. *Paidos* changes in English to *ped,* and therein lies the confusion. There is also a Latin root *ped,* but it does not mean "child"; it means "foot." Thus, though the spelling of these two word elements is the same in English, the meanings are quite different. In most cases the meaning of the element *ped* will be obvious to you, as in the word *pedagogue.* The Greek *agōgos* means "leader"; your good common sense would therefore tell you that it is *children* and not *feet* which are being *led.* A pedagogue is a teacher or leader of children. What do you suppose a demagogue is? Look up the etymology of that word if you don't already know it. Now back to the word *orthopedist.* An orthopedist is one who figuratively *corrects* or *straightens* children. He is specifically a doctor who corrects irregularities of the bones. Since the bones are more malleable in children, he would rather treat his patients in their early years. Now the picture is complete.

The second word whose etymology you should understand is *chiropodist.* This word is built on *cheir* (hand) + *podos* (foot). A chiropodist originally treated both the *hands* and the *feet.* Today, however, a chiropodist no longer treats the hands. His practice is restricted to treating the feet. The word *chiropodist* is currently used interchangeably with the word *podiatrist,* a term whose etymology as well as its definition denotes the treatment of feet only: *podos* (foot) + *iatreia* (healing).

Finally, an *obstetrician* is a doctor who specializes in delivering babies. The word is derived from the Latin *obstetrix*, "midwife," which in turn is derived from *obstare*, "to stand in front of." The word's origin thus suits its modern definition, for the obstetrician literally "stands in front of" the woman when she is giving birth.

cheir (hand) + podos (foot)	= chiropodist
cheir (hand) + practor (one who practices)	= chiropractor
gynē (woman) + logos (study of)	= gynecologist
kardia (heart) + logos (study of)	= cardiology
obstare (to stand before)	= obstetrics
orthos (correct) + odont (tooth)	= orthodontist
orthos (straight) + paidos (child)	= orthopedics
osteon (bone) + pathos (disease)	= osteopath
paidos (child) + iatreia (healing)	= pediatrics
podos (foot) + iatreia (healing)	= podiatry
psychē (mind) + iatreia (healing)	= psychiatry

EXERCISES

A. Complete each sentence by filling in the appropriate word from this lesson.

1. A woman with an ailment common to females would be best treated by a (an) - - - - - .
2. A person whose practice is limited to what he is able to do for his patient with his hands is a (an) - - - - - .
3. You should visit a (an) - - - - - for treatment of curvature of the spine.
4. A (An) - - - - - would put braces on your teeth if necessary.
5. The study of the heart is known as - - - - - .
6. Osteomyelitis, or an inflammation of the bone, might best be treated by a (an) - - - - - .
7. An expectant mother would place herself under the care of a (an) - - - - - .

8. After her child is born, a mother would have a (an) ----- examine the infant.
9. Corns or bunions can best be removed by a (an) ----- or a (an) -----.

B. Write the meaning of each of the two etymons and then write the English word derived from them.

1. paidos ----- + iatreia ----- = -----
2. orthos ----- + odont ----- = -----
3. gynē ----- + logos ----- = -----
4. obstare ----- = -----
5. kardia ----- + logos ----- = -----
6. psychē ----- + iatreia ----- = -----
7. cheir ----- + podos ----- = -----
8. orthos ----- + paidos ----- = -----
9. osteon ----- + pathos ----- = -----
10. podos ----- + iatreia ----- = -----

C. Supply a word from this lesson to fit each definition.

1. a doctor who limits his practice to treating and caring for children
2. a dentist who corrects deformities of the teeth
3. a doctor who treats ailments common only to women
4. a doctor whose practice is limited to delivering babies as well as prenatal care of the prospective mothers
5. a doctor who specializes in the treatment of heart ailments
6. a doctor who specializes in treatment of mental disorders
7. originally, a practitioner in the art of healing the hands and feet; now he treats ailments of the feet only
8. a doctor who specializes in treating and preventing physical deformities (bone malformation, etc.), especially in children
9. a doctor who specializes in treatment of bone diseases
10. a practitioner who adjusts the joints, especially the spine, with his hands

REVIEW EXERCISE: LESSONS 1-30

A. Select the choice that best completes the sentence.

1. An osteopath is concerned with diseases of the (*a*) bones (*b*) pancreas (*c*) skin.
2. To controvert the facts is to (*a*) oppose them (*b*) agree with them (*c*) twist them.
3. A obloquy is a (*a*) funeral oration (*b*) laudatory speech (*c*) verbal attack.
4. An obstreperous child is (*a*) quiet and well-behaved (*b*) sickly (*c*) noisy and unruly.
5. A synonym for the word obtrude is (*a*) extrude (*b*) intrude (*c*) object.
6. Obdurate means (*a*) soft; flexible (*b*) hard; inflexible (*c*) difficult to understand.
7. To oppugn a person's character is to (*a*) praise it (*b*) assail it (*c*) set it as an example.
8. An example of an autocracy would be a (*a*) kingship (*b*) matriarchy (*c*) dictatorship.
9. To decapitate means to (*a*) enumerate (*b*) put at the head (*c*) behead.
10. A gynecologist treats (*a*) bones (*b*) women (*c*) children.
11. A pediatrician treats (*a*) feet (*b*) children (*c*) allergies.
12. Inadvertent means (*a*) unintentional (*b*) careful (*c*) impolite.

B. Write a brief definition of each etymon.

1. vertere
2. cheir
3. osteon
4. ob
5. loqui
6. caedere
7. noxa
8. pugnare
9. claudere
10. autos

C. Select the etymon for which the definition is given.

1. all: (*a*) poly (*b*) pan (*c*) tauto (*d*) pro
2. kind; origin; race; birth: (*a*) dēmos (*b*) hopla (*c*) genos (*d*) chrōma
3. self: (*a*) sōma (*b*) syn (*c*) homo (*d*) autos
4. rule or government: (*a*) sophos (*b*) kratos (*c*) dēlos (*d*) gōnia
5. not; without: (*a*) a (*b*) ana (*c*) pyr (*d*) em
6. feeling; disease: (*a*) doxa (*b*) kakos (*c*) opsis (*d*) pathos
7. true: (*a*) fatus (*b*) uxor (*c*) verus (*d*) auspex
8. people: (*a*) dēmos (*b*) dendron (*c*) dermis (*d*) dipsa
9. god: (*a*) logos (*b*) theos (*c*) sophos (*d*) xylon
10. marriage: (*a*) gynē (*b*) archon (*c*) gamos (*d*) andros
11. well: (*a*) pan (*b*) epi (*c*) topos (*d*) eu
12. love: (*a*) philos (*b*) phobos (*c*) haima (*d*) paidos
13. many: (*a*) poly (*b*) peri (*c*) milli (*d*) hieros
14. to kill: (*a*) claudere (*b*) mittere (*c*) caedere (*d*) ponere
15. head: (*a*) ars (*b*) caput (*c*) lingua (*d*) venter
16. to point or prick: (*a*) flectere (*b*) punct (*c*) perspicere (*d*) sidēre
17. foot: (*a*) podos (*b*) cheir (*c*) ichthys (*d*) paidos
18. child: (*a*) paidos (*b*) podos (*c*) taphos (*d*) lexikos
19. known: (*a*) iatreia (*b*) odynē (*c*) tēle (*d*) gnōstos
20. man (mankind): (*a*) archon (*b*) anthrōpos (*c*) agora (*d*) aristos

LESSON 31

specere to look or see

The Latin *specere*, meaning "to look or see," is an etymon of many English words. Words containing the elements *spic*, *spec*, or *spect* are usually derived from *specere.*

Perspicacious comes from the Latin *per* (through) + *specere* (to see). It is an adjective which characterizes a person of keen mental discernment. You can't hoodwink the perspicacious mind, for it is like a powerful searchlight. It would *see through* the deception in the twinkling of an eye.

Perspicuous is built on the same two Latin words as *perspicacious*; but whereas *perspicacious* applies to mental perception, *perspicuous* refers to the thing perceived. An argument is perspicuous if it is clear, unobscure, and unambiguous. A perspicuous statement is therefore *seen through*, or understood, because of its clarity and lucidity.

The word *specious* comes from the Latin *speciocus* (good-looking). The Latin word acquired the sense "deceptively good-looking," and it is that sense which passed into the English *specious.* Reasoning which is specious sounds plausible and correct, but is in fact faulty.

Finally, the word *auspicious* comes from the Latin *auspex*, meaning "one who predicts the future by observing birds." *Au* derives from *avis*, the Latin word for "bird." In ancient times prophecies were often made by diviners or seers from observation of the entrails of birds. Hence from *auspex* is derived the word *auspicious*, meaning "of good omen, or constituting a favorable sign."

ad (at) + specere	= aspect
avis (bird) + specere	= auspicious
intro (within) + specere	= introspection
per (through) + specere	= perspicacious

male (evil; bad) + facere =
+ or (one who) = malefactor; malefic
manus (hand) + facere = manufacture
omnis (all) + facere = omnific
beneficent
facile (used or comprehended with ease)
facilitate
factitious (artificial)
proficient

EXERCISES

A. Complete each sentence by filling in the appropriate word from this lesson.

1. The handyman responded to the ad which called for a (an) ------.
2. Archeologists have uncovered many ----- that attest to the artistic skill of prehistoric man.
3. The orphaned child's ----- who made gifts to him at Christmas wished to remain anonymous.
4. The ----- of prayer has often been called into question by unbelievers.
5. Because she was a (an) ----- worker, the management kept her on during the slack season.
6. It certainly was an amazingly good ----- of the original painting.
7. The witch doctor pronounced a (an) ----- curse on the itinerant missionary.
8. God is not only omniscient, or all-knowing, but also -----, or able to do all things.

B. Select the choice that best completes the sentence or answers the question.

1. A person who did you a service in your hour of need would be your (*a*) malefactor (*b*) factotum (*c*) benefactor.

per (through) + specere = perspicuous
pro (forward) + specere = prospectus
retro (back) + specere = retrospect
sub (under; secretly) + specere = suspect
conspicuous (obvious; noticeable)
specious
spectator
specter (visible spirit; ghost)
spectroscope (instrument that measures visible light)
spectrum (visible light range)

EXERCISES

A. Match each definition in column A with the correct word in column B.

Column A	*Column B*
1. appearance; view	*a.* prospectus
2. favorable; propitious	*b.* aspect
3. advance information made known to arouse interest	*c.* perspicuous
4. apparition; visible spirit	*d.* perspicacious
5. looking within one's own mind	*e.* specter
6. appearing to be genuine or true without being so	*f.* introspection
7. clear; lucid; unambiguous	*g.* retrospect
8. marked by keen mental discernment	*h.* suspect
9. a look back	*i.* auspicious
10. to mistrust; have doubts of	*j.* specious

B. Complete each sentence by filling in the appropriate word from this lesson.

1. At the seance, the woman swore that she saw a (an) ----- whose countenance resembled that of her late husband.

2. -----, or self-examination, is good for the soul; many of our shortcomings become apparent to us.
3. To examine our lives in ----- often makes us acutely aware of past mistakes which could have been avoided.
4. The salesman's ----- argument for buying the compact car did not fool me, though it did sound plausible.
5. His proposal was so ----- and well thought out that the committee praised it for its clarity.
6. The murder investigation took on the ----- of a grimly bizarre game of wits being played by the detective and the murderer.
7. His ----- mind anticipated my every move.
8. It was a (an) ----- breeze which carried the shipwrecked sailors to the safety of a small inhabited island.
9. I ----- that you are trying to win me over to your cause through a specious kind of reasoning.
10. The company forwarded to all its stockholders a (an) ----- anticipating the year's dividends and capital gains.

C. Write *T* if the sentence is true and *F* if it is false.

1. A *spectator* is one who gambles on the stock market.
2. An *auspicious* occasion is one which is not in any way noteworthy.
3. To look in *retrospect* upon an event is to look back on it.
4. *Introspection* is an important part of many religions, especially religions that emphasize the moral life.
5. A *perspicuous* remark is more often than not tasteless and offensive in its content.
6. A chess player marked by a *perspicacious* mind would present to you a formidable opponent.
7. Most excellent debaters have practiced the art of *specious* reasoning, since it is so vital to effective debate.
8. A rainbow displays many colors of the *spectrum*.
9. A *spectroscope* is an instrument for observing specters.

LESSON 32

facere to make; do

The Latin word *facere* means "to make or do." In English has variant forms of spelling, including *fac*, *fic*, and *fec*. *Facere* one of the ten most common etymons in the English languag Hence it should not be a surprise to you that the Latin *facere* a its variant spellings help to build hundreds of words in our languag In the following list, definitions have been provided where et mologies do not make the meanings clear.

Two words, however, may require an additional commer That which is *efficacious* has an intended effect, or "works"; usually apply the word to actions or attempts, rather than to pe sons. Thus, we say that prayers are efficacious, or that a certa medicine is efficacious. *Proficient* is applied to persons, and sugges not only accomplishment, but a high degree of skill as well: thu "she was proficient in her work; he was proficient in four la guages."

ars (skill) + facere	= artifact (art object made by hand)
ars (skill) + facere	= artifice (ingenious device or expedient)
bene (good; well) + facere + or (one who)	= benefactor
de (away) + facere	= defect (blemish); defector (one who turns away from a group or cause); deficient (lacking)
ex (out) + facere	= efficacy; efficacious (having power to produce intended effects)
facere + similis (like)	= facsimile
facere + totus (all)	= factotum (a handyman)

2. An example of a malefactor would be a (*a*) judge (*b*) criminal (*c*) teacher.
3. If you advertised for a handyman, you would expect which of the following to apply for the job?
(*a*) a malefactor (*b*) a benefactor (*c*) a factotum
4. Were you to buy an art object advertised as an original, you would be sadly disappointed to learn that it was only a (*a*) factotum (*b*) malefic (*c*) facsimile.
5. Having taken a medicine, you would expect it to have what kind of effect on you?
(*a*) malefic (*b*) maleficent (*c*) efficacious
6. He had great difficulty writing, but his speech was always (*a*) malefic (*b*) maleficent (*c*) facile.

C. Write the meaning of each etymon used with *facere* and then write the English word derived from *facere* + the etymon.

1. facere + similis ----- = -----
2. facere + totus ----- = -----
3. ars ----- + facere = -----
4. male ----- + facere = -----
5. bene ----- + facere = -----
6. manus ----- + facere = -----
7. omnis ----- + facere = -----
8. ex ----- + facere = -----

LESSON 33

graphein to write

The Greek word *graphein* is another of the ten most common etymons in the English language. It contributes to a great number of words whose meanings are probably well-known. The words presented below are not quite so well-known to most people. Keep in mind that the acquisition of new words themselves is not as valuable to you as the learning of the etymons which go to make up these words.

autos (self) + bios (life) + graphein	= autobiography
biblion (book) + graphein	= bibliography
carte (map) + graphein	= cartography
dēmos (people) + graphein	= demography
epi (upon) + graphein	= epigraphy
hydōr (water) + graphein	= hydrography
kakos (bad) + graphein	= cacography (recall *cacophony*)
kalos (beautiful) + graphein	= calligraphy
lexikos (of words) + graphein	= lexicographer (lexicon)
multus (many) + graphein	= multigraph
orthos (correct) + graphein	= orthography
pornē (harlot) + graphein	= pornography
seismos (earthquake) + graphein	= seismograph
topos (place) + graphein	= topography

Note: The word *graffito*, whose plural form is *graffiti*, means "a rude inscription, such as might be found scrawled on sidewalks, building walls, or large rocks." *Epigraphy*, on the other hand, means "the study of inscriptions," and applies to any kind of inscriptions, whether "rude" or not.

EXERCISES

A. Complete each word by filling in the required word fragment derived from one of the etymons you have studied.

1. -----graphy = person's life story written by himself
2. -----graphy = list of books or writings on a given subject
3. -----graphy = art of map-making
4. -----graphy = study of bodies of water
5. -----grapher = one who works at preparing dictionaries
6. -----graphy = study of population
7. -----graphy = depiction of erotic behavior intended to cause sexual excitement
8. -----graph = duplicating machine
9. -----graphy = surveying physical features or contours on the earth's surface
10. -----graph = instrument which records the intensity of earth tremors

B. Select the word that best completes the sentence.

1. A sea captain would be vitally concerned with (*a*) orthography (*b*) topography (*c*) hydrography.
2. A person running office machines would probably be acquainted with a (an) (*a*) multigraph (*b*) orthograph (*c*) epigraph.
3. A scholarly work usually lists sources or contains (*a*) an autobiography (*b*) a bibliography (*c*) a demography.
4. Since the Department of Health, Education and Welfare is vitally concerned with population trends, it conducts studies in (*a*) epigraphy (*b*) demography (*c*) orthography.
5. Sociological clues to the actions and thoughts of groups of people may be found in (*a*) seismography (*b*) graffiti (*c*) lexicography.
6. A linguist would probably be well versed in (*a*) demography (*b*) calligraphy (*c*) orthography.

7. The word *topography* would be used extensively by a (*a*) doctor (*b*) surveyor (*c*) printer.
8. A geologist would be familiar with the term (*a*) orthography (*b*) calligraphy (*c*) seismograph.
9. Carl Sandburg wrote an excellent account of Lincoln's life; he wrote Lincoln's (*a*) biography (*b*) autobiography (*c*) bibliography.
10. One of the archeologist's primary areas of study would be (*a*) epigraphy (*b*) lexicography (*c*) cacography.

C. Write the meaning of each etymon used with *graphein* and then write the English word derived from *graphein* + the etymon.

1. lexikos ----- + graphein = -----
2. orthos ----- + graphein = -----
3. pornē ----- + graphein = -----
4. seismos ----- + graphein = -----
5. carte ----- + graphein = -----
6. biblion ----- + graphein = -----
7. autos ----- + bios ----- + graphein = -----
8. dēmos ----- + graphein = -----
9. multus ----- + graphein = -----
10. topos ----- + graphein = -----

LESSON 34

mikros small

makros long; large

The Greek words *mikros* and *makros* are opposite in meaning. The former means "small," the latter "large." Many English words derived from *mikros* or *makros* are of a technical nature. Once again, do not be overly concerned with words as such—that is, with word lists. It is method which should be of vital concern to you. Learn the etymologies, and vocabulary building will take care of itself.

makros + graphein (to write) = macrograph
makros + kosmos (world; universe) = macrocosm
makros + skopein (to view) = macroscopic
macron (symbol used to designate long vowel sound, as in "ē")

mikros + bios (life) = microbe
mikros + bios (life) + caedere (to kill) = microbicide
mikros + fy (suffix meaning to make) = micrify
mikros + graphein (to write) = micrograph
mikros + kosmos (world) = microcosm
mikros + metron (measure) = micrometer
mikros + phōnē (sound) = microphone
mikros + skopein (to view) = microscope
micron (1/1000th part of one millimeter)

EXERCISES

A. Match each definition in column A with the correct word from column B.

Column A	*Column B*
1. symbol used to designate a long vowel sound	*a.* micrify
2. one thousandth of a millimeter	*b.* macrocosm
3. agent that kills living cells (germs)	*c.* micrograph
4. instrument used to measure minute distances	*d.* micron
5. visible to the naked eye	*e.* microbicide
6. community or institution which epitomizes the world; little world	*f.* microbe
7. universe	*g.* micrometer
8. to make small	*h.* macroscopic
9. instrument for very fine writing or engraving	*i.* macron
10. germ; disease organism which is not visible to the naked eye	*j.* microcosm

B. Complete each word by filling in the required word fragment derived from one of the etymons you have studied.

1. micro----- = not visible to naked eye

2. macro----- = universe

3. macro----- = visible to the naked eye

4. micr----- = to make small or insignificant

5. micro----- = one thousandth of a millimeter

6. micro----- = that which kills germs

7. macro----- = symbol that designates a long vowel sound

8. micro----- = germ

9. micro----- = small world

10. micro----- = instrument for executing fine writing

C. Select the correct definition of each etymon.

1. kosmos: (*a*) marketplace (*b*) world (*c*) law (*d*) rock
2. bios: (*a*) death (*b*) shape (*c*) life (*d*) view
3. metron: (*a*) measure (*b*) sound (*c*) world (*d*) wealth
4. phōnē: (*a*) nation (*b*) tongue (*c*) worship (*d*) sound
5. skopein: (*a*) to write (*b*) to view (*c*) to cut (*d*) to measure
6. caedere: (*a*) to shut (*b*) to devour (*c*) to kill (*d*) to correct
7. graphein: (*a*) to write (*b*) to rule (*c*) to love (*d*) to speak
8. makros: (*a*) small (*b*) measure (*c*) world (*d*) large
9. mikros: (*a*) large (*b*) hatred (*c*) time (*d*) small

LESSON 35

dicere to say; speak; tell

capere to take

Many of the words derived from the Latin etymons *dicere* and *capere* are well known to you. In addition, many of the etymons that commonly combine with *dicere* or *capere* to form modern English words will be familiar to you if you have completed the other lessons in this section. In many cases the meaning of *capere* has been extended until the original sense of "to take" is all but lost in the English derivative. Words derived from *dicere*, on the other hand, usually retain the idea of "saying" or "telling." Use your imagination to try to determine how each word got its present meaning.

bene (well) + dicere	= benediction
contra (against) + dicere	= contradict
e (out) + dicere	= edict
inter (between; among) + dicere	= interdict (prohibit)
male (bad) + dicere	= malediction
dicere + or (one who)	= dictator
dicere + phōnē (sound)	= dictaphone
dictation	
diction	
dictionary	
dictum (an authoritative statement)	
con (together; with) + capere	= conceive; conception
contra (against) + capere	= contraception
de (against) + capere	= deceive; deception
in (in) + capere	= inception

re (back) + capere = receive; reception; recipient

capacious (roomy)
caption
captious (taking issue on insignificant points)
captivate

EXERCISES

A. Match each word in column A with its definition in column B.

Column A	*Column B*
1. edict	*a.* title
2. diction	*b.* charm
3. inception	*c.* reading aloud of words to be written by another
4. caption	*d.* official proclamation
5. dictum	*e.* prohibit
6. captivate	*f.* trick
7. conception	*g.* use of words
8. interdict	*h.* idea
9. deception	*i.* authoritative pronouncement
10. dictation	*j.* origin

B. Complete each sentence by filling in the appropriate word from the following list:

caption	captious	edict	capacious
interdict	captivate	diction	benediction
	recipient	dictator	

1. A royal ----- announced the end of military rule.

2. The priest closed the religious service by uttering a (an) -----.

3. A government ruled by a (an) ----- cannot tolerate opposition.

4. An actor must have excellent ----- in order to be understood from the back of the auditorium.
5. The federal government has power to ----- the shipment of certain goods across state lines.
6. The ----- of a paycheck must endorse the check before it can be cashed.
7. In order to understand the cartoon, one had to read the ----- below it.
8. Occasionally a biased literary critic tries to discredit a well-written book by resorting to many ----- arguments against it.
9. The ----- moving van easily contained all the furniture in the house.
10. Puppies in a pet shop window invariably ----- young passers-by.

REVIEW EXERCISE: LESSONS 31-35

Since this is the last review lesson in this section, you will concern yourself with the last five lessons, 31 through 35. Immediately following, there will be a mastery test covering all the lessons in the section.

A. Select the word that best completes the sentence.

1. To look back on events is to view them in (*a*) introspect (*b*) retrospect (*c*) aspect.
2. That which prevents conception is a (*a*) contraceptive (*b*) perceptive (*c*) receptive.
3. A germ is a (*a*) macrobe (*b*) microbe (*c*) microcosm.
4. To make small or minute is to (*a*) micrify (*b*) macrify (*c*) microbe.
5. That which has an evil or bad effect is (*a*) beneficent (*b*) malefic (*c*) maledict.
6. A criminal is a (*a*) malefactor (*b*) benefactor (*c*) factotum.

7. Looking within one's own mind is called (*a*) retrospection (*b*) prospection (*c*) introspection.
8. A false argument which appears sound and just is (*a*) specious (*b*) auspicious (*c*) perspicacious.
9. To produce an intended effect, a medicine would have to be (*a*) malefic (*b*) benevolent (*c*) efficacious.
10. The universe or world is called the (*a*) microcosm (*b*) macrocosm (*c*) cosmopolitan.

B. Write *T* if the sentence is true and *F* if it is false.

1. The Greek word element *makros* means large.
2. A person with a *perspicacious* mind is not easily taken in by propaganda.
3. A *specious* argument by a propagandist could easily convince you if you were not on your guard.
4. A perspicacious mind would be likely to contrive a *perspicuous* argument.
5. A *pedagogue* is a political leader of people.
6. A *factotum* is a good person to have around when something needs fixing.
7. A geologist would know the meaning of the word *seismograph*.
8. The study of inscriptions is called *epigraphy*.
9. That which destroys germs is known as a *microbicide*.
10. An *aspect* is an obstacle or an obstruction.

C. Write a brief definition of each etymon.

1. specere
2. mikros
3. makros
4. facere
5. graphein
6. phōnē
7. metron
8. orthos
9. epi
10. paidos

MASTERY TEST: LESSONS 1-35

You have come to the end of one stage of a long and eventful journey into the world of words. How well did you master the etymologies presented in this section? The following mastery test will answer the question. Perhaps you would like to review before starting your mastery test. It is advisable that you do so; however, should you feel a review unnecessary, please proceed as directed.

A. Write a brief definition of each etymon listed below.

1. pan
2. genos
3. poly
4. multus
5. hyper
6. hypo
7. inter
8. intra
9. a; an
10. pre
11. circum
12. scribere
13. specere
14. loqui
15. temnein
16. phobos
17. pathos
18. vertere
19. anthrōpos
20. contra
21. caput
22. chrōma
23. caedere
24. autos
25. gamos
26. makros
27. gynē
28. kratos
29. archon
30. theos
31. skopein
32. morphē
33. male
34. dicere
35. facere
36. phōnē
37. gnōstos
38. dēmos
39. graphein
40. philos
41. logos
42. eu
43. mania
44. podos
45. orthos
46. anima
47. retro
48. intro
49. sophos
50. psychē

B. Complete each word by filling in the required word fragment derived from one of the etymons you have studied.

1. pan_ _ _ _ _atic = sensitive to light of all colors
2. geno_ _ _ _ _ = destruction of a racial, political, or religious group
3. psycho_ _ _ _ _ = originating in the mind
4. _ _ _ _ _geneous = of different kinds
5. _ _ _ _ _acious = garrulous; talkative
6. _ _ _ _ _locution = talking in circles
7. _ _ _ _ _diction = a curse
8. ana_ _ _ _ _ = thing misplaced in time
9. a_ _ _ _ _ = one who professes ignorance in matters of religion
10. a_ _ _ _ _ = doctrine that God does not exist
11. _ _ _ _ _theism = belief in many gods
12. poly_ _ _ _ _ = one who speaks many languages
13. _ _ _ _ _anthropist = one who loves mankind
14. _ _ _ _ _chromatic = having many colors
15. _ _ _ _ _logy = speech of praise
16. caco_ _ _ _ _ = harsh, discordant sound
17. pusill_ _ _ _ _ = weak of spirit; cowardly
18. magn_ _ _ _ _ = generous; lofty; noble
19. psycho_ _ _ _ _ = one whose mind is deranged
20. a_ _ _ _ _ = lack of feeling; indifference

C. Select the word that best fits each definition.

1. no name: (*a*) synonym (*b*) anonym (*c*) pseudonym
2. without color: (*a*) aphonic (*b*) anachronistic (*c*) achromatic
3. dictatorial rule: (*a*) autonomy (*b*) autocracy (*c*) aristocracy
4. man who makes love triflingly: (*a*) philanthropist (*b*) philanderer (*c*) bibliophile

5. a curse: (*a*) malefactor (*b*) maladroit (*c*) malediction
6. monologue: (*a*) obloquy (*b*) soliloquy (*c*) colloquy
7. wide, extensive view: (*a*) pandemic (*b*) panorama (*c*) panacea
8. interracial marriage: (*a*) miscegenation (*b*) heterogeneous (*c*) eugenics
9. doctrine that God is in everything: (*a*) pansophism (*b*) pantology (*c*) pantheism
10. practice of producing a superior strain through inbreeding: (*a*) euphony (*b*) eugenics (*c*) autogeny
11. killing painlessly: (*a*) euthanasia (*b*) genocide (*c*) uxoricide
12. defamatory speech: (*a*) eulogy (*b*) panegyric (*c*) obloquy
13. noisy; unruly: (*a*) obdurate (*b*) obstreperous (*c*) obese
14. having a keen mind: (*a*) perspicuous (*b*) perspicacious (*c*) pervicacious
15. one who hates mankind: (*a*) philanthropist (*b*) anthropologist (*c*) misanthrope
16. to go against; oppose: (*a*) circumscribe (*b*) contract (*c*) controvert
17. strong feeling against; aversion: (*a*) pathology (*b*) apathy (*c*) antipathy
18. to serve as a typical or ideal example: (*a*) dichotomize (*b*) ostracize (*c*) epitomize
19. transfer of feelings: (*a*) apathy (*b*) antipathy (*c*) empathy
20. in the flesh; personified: (*a*) carnal (*b*) carrion (*c*) incarnate
21. to prevent, block, or impede: (*a*) precocious (*b*) prerogative (*c*) preclude
22. preference or predisposition: (*a*) antecedent (*b*) predilection (*c*) precursor
23. to limit: (*a*) circumscribe (*b*) circumlocution (*c*) circumvent

24. right attached to rank, royalty, or office: (*a*) predilection (*b*) prescience (*c*) prerogative
25. one who is turned within himself: (*a*) intravert (*b*) intromit (*c*) introvert

D. Complete each sentence by filling in the appropriate word from the following list.

miscegenation	irrevocable	prerogative
anachronistic	anomaly	animated
preclude	pantheism	psychogenic
inadvertently	malefactor	retrospect
panegyric	gynecologist	autonomy
euthanasia	monogamy	philanthropic
loquacious	panoramic	

1. The poet wrote a (an) ----- lauding the endeavors of Oliver Cromwell.
2. John ------ spilled his glass of milk on Mary's new dress.
3. ----- is the prevailing pattern of marriage in our culture.
4. The ----- attorney's summation speech to the jury was three hours long.
5. Many diseases or ailments common only to women can best be treated by a (an) -----.
6. Looking upon the proceedings in -----, one could easily determine the cause of failure.
7. Many African nations gained ----- only recently.
8. In order to ----- his being captured alive, the spy swallowed poison contained in a hidden vial.
9. Marriage between two people of different races is known as -----.
10. Many teen-agers believe their parents' views on dating are outmoded and -----.
11. ----- is a religious belief that embraces nature worship.
12. The ----- was brought before a court of justice and was found guilty of the crime.

13. Although he had said that his decision to resign was -----, he now changed his mind and announced that he would remain in office.
14. There are many ------ charities which work toward the goal of the betterment of mankind.
15. From the top of the mountain we had a (an) ----- view of the entire valley.
16. Many illnesses are not physical in origin, but rather -----.
17. A (An) ----- discussion was taking place, with arms gesticulating frantically.
18. The executive ----- to veto bills passed by the legislature is one of the checks and balances found in our democracy.
19. Talking animals appear frequently in children's stories, but in real life they would be a (an) -----.
20. When a horse with a broken leg is destroyed, we refer to the killing as -----, or a painless death.

The Third Dimension

Related Words

So far you have studied two methods for learning new words. One of these methods is the study of *interesting word histories.* The other is the study of *etymologies.* A third way to learn words is by association with other *words related to the same general idea.*

The words in each lesson in this part have a general idea in common. Within a given lesson may be found together synonyms, approximate synonyms, and words only loosely related by the idea they have in common. The definitions provided are intentionally brief and general. Do not rely on the definition alone in learning a new word. In the normal use of language we are called upon to supply the appropriate word in context, not to define. The illustrative sentence is therefore as important as the definition, for it shows how the word is used in context. It goes without saying that a good dictionary should always be at hand to resolve any uncertainties you may have about a word.

LESSON 1

You probably have a friend or an acquaintance who talks incessantly or who writes letters of interminable length. Where does he get the energy? There is a host of words which aptly characterize such a *talkative* or *wordy* person. Listed below are examples of such words, which are, incidentally, all adjectives. Say each word to yourself several times before going on to the exercise.

garrulous talking much; long-winded (*adj.*)

The *garrulous* celebrity on the television "talk" program was silenced only by the commercial.

loquacious given to talking; garrulous (*adj.*)

His wife was as *loquacious* as he was taciturn.

prolix wordy; verbose (*adj.*)

Man, who has been accorded the gift of speech, often abuses this God-given talent by indulging in *prolix* conversations, much to the anguish of his audience.

verbose abounding in words; prolix; wordy (*adj.*)

Much student writing in its attempt to sound sophisticated ends by being only *verbose.*

vociferous loud; implies vehement shouting (*adj.*)

The *vociferous* debate proceeded on the premise that he who shouted loudest had the best cause.

voluble glib; garrulous (*adj.*)

After being subjected to an hour-long harangue by his political opponent, the mayor referred to his antagonist as a "worthy though *voluble* foe."

EXERCISE

From the following list of words, select those that are related to the general idea "talkative or wordy":

1. didactic
2. prolix
3. abstruse
4. voracious
5. mellifluous
6. laconic
7. loquacious
8. erudite
9. verbose
10. tacit
11. garrulous
12. vicarious
13. dissident
14. exoteric
15. voluble

LESSON 2

"It's always darkest before the dawn."

"Nothing succeeds like success."

"A bird in the hand is worth two in the bush."

You are no doubt familiar with equivalent expressions common to your own geographic area. Such expressions enjoy a common denominator: they are all *short* and *moralistic*, or *proverbial*, *sayings*. In addition, they are often well-known sayings that have enjoyed long use. Such expressions are known by many names. Examine carefully the following words, which are all nouns.

adage old, familiar saying; proverb (*n.*)

The venerable *adage* "Do unto others as you would have them do unto you" was rejected by George Bernard Shaw on the ground that people's standards differ.

anodyne expression intended to lift the spirits (*n.*)

"Prosperity is just around the corner" was a popular *anodyne* of the depression era of the 1930's.

aphorism short, pithy saying (*n.*)

The *aphorism* "Brevity is the soul of wit" has much to offer prolix storytellers.

apothegm striking or witty aphorism (*n.*)

Modern psychology has confirmed the truth of Thoreau's *apothegm*, "The mass of men lead lives of quiet desperation."

dictum authoritative pronouncement (*n.*)

The moral *dictum* "Thou shalt not kill" cannot be reconciled with the killing which occurs in time of war.

maxim precept; rule of thumb (*n.*)

Benjamin Franklin's *maxim* "Time is money" is no less true today than it was two hundred years ago.

parable short, moralistic narrative (*n.*)

Many worthwhile moral lessons can be gotten from reading the *parables* found in the Bible.

truism undoubted or self-evident truth (*n.*)

"Crime does not pay" is a *truism* which many convicted criminals wish they had heeded.

EXERCISES

A. Select from the following list of words those that are related to the general idea "a short, moralistic saying; a proverb."

1. apothegm
2. prosthesis
3. hyperbole
4. anodyne
5. maxim
6. acronym
7. aphorism
8. denouement
9. parable
10. polemic
11. syndrome
12. truism
13. tautology
14. adage
15. dictum

B. Supply the missing letters to complete a word related to the general idea "talkative or wordy."

1. l-----
2. g-----
3. p-----
4. v-----
5. v-----
6. v-----

C. Supply the missing letters to complete a word that fits the definition.

1. talkative l-----
2. self-evident truth t-----
3. wordy v-----
4. proverbial saying m-----

5. talkative v-----
6. loud; boisterous v-----
7. long-winded; wordy p-----
8. narrative from which a moral is drawn p-----
9. expression intended to ease mental anguish a-----
10. pithy saying a-----

LESSON 3

There are many words in English which convey the idea of *secrecy*. The secrecy denoted in such words may be premeditated or entirely without design. After becoming sufficiently acquainted with each of the following words, continue your study by doing the exercises.

clandestine conducted with secrecy by design, usually for illicit purposes (*adj.*)

The conspirators arranged a *clandestine* meeting to plot against Caesar.

covert covered over; private; hidden (*adj.*)

The gems were stolen despite the fact that the jeweler kept them in a *covert* place.

esoteric known or understood by only a few (*adj.*)

Albert Einstein's *esoteric* views on the nature of the universe are almost impossible for the lay person to comprehend.

furtive done by stealth; hence, sly (*adj.*)

The thief cast *furtive* glances about as he heard approaching footsteps.

obfuscate to confuse by design (in order to keep something from others) (*v.t.*)

By *obfuscating* the issue, the dishonest mayor believed that he could hide the truth.

recondite difficult to comprehend (*adj.*)

The professor's *recondite* paper on atomic fission was published in 1947.

sub rosa privately; confidentially (*adv.*)

The meeting between the two foreign agents in enemy territory was conducted *sub rosa.*

surreptitious clandestine; stealthy (*adj.*)

Investigations revealed that the city official had made several *surreptitious* business deals.

EXERCISES

A. Select from the following list of words those that are related to the general idea "secret or hidden."

1. vapid
2. covert
3. effete
4. esoteric
5. nefarious
6. surreptitious
7. sinister
8. obfuscate
9. recondite
10. spurious
11. saturnine
12. sub rosa
13. furtive
14. trivial
15. clandestine

B. Supply the missing letters to complete a word related to the general idea "proverb or saying."

1. a_ _ _ _ _
2. m_ _ _ _ _
3. t_ _ _ _ _
4. d_ _ _ _ _
5. p_ _ _ _ _
6. a_ _ _ _ _
7. a_ _ _ _ _
8. a_ _ _ _ _

C. Supply the missing letters to complete a word that fits the definition.

1. conducted with secrecy by design c_ _ _ _ _
2. loud; boisterous v_ _ _ _ _
3. moralistic narrative p_ _ _ _ _
4. done with stealth by design s_ _ _ _ _

5. sly; stealthy f-----

6. expression intended to ease mental anguish a-----

7. self-evident truth t-----

8. difficult to comprehend; abstruse r-----

9. withheld from open avowal; abstruse e-----

10. long-winded; protracted, as a speech p-----

11. private; hidden c-----

12. talkative g-----

13. talkative l-----

14. authoritative pronouncement d-----

15. privately; confidentially s----- -----

LESSON 4

In this lesson you will study a group of words which have as a common denominator *time.* More specifically, these words refer to an action, event, or happening which takes place *before* another action. Read each definition and illustrative sentence carefully before going on to the exercises.

antecedent that which goes before in time (*n.*)

Our modern alphabet has *antecedents* in the Greek and Phoenician alphabets.

augur to foretell as from omens (*v.t.*)

Many people believe that top secret documents *augured* the coming of the Japanese attack on Pearl Harbor.

harbinger forerunner; precursor; something that foreshadows what is to come (*n.*)

In many parts of the United States the robin is thought to be spring's *harbinger.*

precursor one that precedes; forerunner; one that prepares the way for another (*n.*)

American and Russian satellites successfully launched in the 1950's were *precursors* of man's eventual space travel.

prelude introductory action before the main matter (*n.*)

Hitler's advent to power in Germany was the *prelude* to World War II.

presage to foretell; predict (*v.t.*)

In Shakespeare's *Julius Caesar*, the soothsayer *presaged* Caesar's assassination when he warned Caesar to "beware the ides of March."

presage presentiment; foreboding (*n.*)

The superstitious person regards simple fears as *presages* of ill fortune.

prognosticate to predict; forecast; prophesy (*v.t.*)

Phrases such as "chance of" and "probability" enable weathermen to *prognosticate* the weather with impunity.

vanguard that which is in the forefront (*n.*)

The troops which acted as a *vanguard* for the division following them were ambushed and wiped out.

EXERCISES

A. Select from the following list of words those that are related to the general idea of "coming before another action or event in time."

1. vanguard
2. prognosticate
3. accolade
4. presage
5. antecedent
6. sibling
7. augur
8. rue
9. harbinger
10. scapegoat
11. canard
12. innuendo
13. quintessence
14. prelude
15. precursor

B. Supply the missing letters to complete a word related to the general idea "secret or hidden."

1. r_ _ _ _ _
2. e_ _ _ _ _
3. c_ _ _ _ _
4. f_ _ _ _ _
5. s_ _ _ _ _
6. c_ _ _ _ _
7. s_ _ _ _ _ r_ _ _ _ _
8. o_ _ _ _ _

C. Match each definition in column A with the correct word from column B.

Column A	*Column B*
1. expression intended to ease mental anguish	*a.* prelude
2. saying whose meaning is too obvious to mention	*b.* prolix
3. secretly; in confidence	*c.* parable
4. to predict as from omens	*d.* anodyne
5. sly; wary	*e.* esoteric
6. wordy; verbose	*f.* sub rosa
7. understood by only a select few	*g.* precursor
8. harbinger; forerunner	*h.* vociferous
9. event preceding the main action	*i.* augur
10. short narrative from which a moral can be drawn	*j.* furtive
11. loud; boisterous	*k.* truism

LESSON 6

The English language contains a profusion of words that convey the idea of *assailing with verbal abuse*. It is indeed sad that we need a multitude of such words to express our dislike or even hatred of people or institutions. Nevertheless, we should learn these words, for they are used quite extensively.

calumniate to accuse falsely or maliciously of a crime (*v.t.*)

Hitler's propaganda machine *calumniated* the Jews in an attempt to condone their extermination.

denigrate to blacken; defame (*v.t.*)

There is hardly an important political figure whose name has not been *denigrated* by a malcontent minority group.

imprecation curse (*n.*)

The collision of the truck with the taxi was followed by a hearty exchange of *imprecations*.

impugn to assail by words; oppose as false (*v.t.*)

The communist bloc nations are noted for their official statements *impugning* the motives of United States foreign policy.

inveigh to utter severe denunciations; declaim bitterly (*v.i.*; always followed by "against")

In a deplorable situation it is better to weigh the facts and then take a positive corrective action than to simply sit back and *inveigh* against it.

malign to speak evil of; traduce (*v.t.*)

An old tactic of political candidates is to *malign* the opposition.

LESSON 5

The English language contains a host of words which denote an *abundance*, *much*, or *many*. Below is a partial listing of such words. Study the definitions and the illustrative sentences carefully to determine the proper context for each word.

array imposing series of things (*n.*)

The display featured a large *array* of cut flowers.

galaxy assemblage of noted persons or things (*n.*)

A *galaxy* of movie stars turned out for the gala premiere.

legion great number; multitude (*n.*; usually used without an article)

The purposes and aims of education are *legion*; perhaps this is one reason for its present confused condition.

manifold numerous and varied (*adj.*)

Some doctors believe the agents of cancer are *manifold*, while others feel the disease results from a single virus.

multitude state of being many; numerousness (*n.*)

There is a *multitude* of reasons which should dissuade one from smoking.

profusion abundance; lavish supply (*n.*)

The *profusion* of summer flowers created for me the illusion of a tropical island.

sundry several; various; divers (*adj.*)

There are various and *sundry* factors contributing to the existence of juvenile delinquency.

EXERCISES

A. Select from the following list of words those that are related to the general idea "a great number; an abundance."

1. fiasco
2. legion
3. nonpareil
4. iota
5. array
6. symposium
7. sundry
8. holocaust
9. multitude
10. paraplegia
11. profusion
12. anthology
13. alms
14. galaxy
15. manifold

B. Supply the missing letters to complete a word related to the general idea "going before or saying beforehand."

1. p-----
2. a-----
3. p-----
4. h-----
5. v-----
6. p-----
7. a-----
8. p-----

C. Select the word that is closest in meaning to the italicized word or phrase.

1. The florist offered his customers a *large assortment* of floral pieces, both live and artificial.
   (*a*) profusion (*b*) harbinger (*c*) truism (*d*) parable
2. Some apathetic voters give *many and various* reasons for not fulfilling their citizenship obligation.
   (*a*) esoteric (*b*) furtive (*c*) sundry (*d*) vociferous
3. The *great number* of crimes committed in poor neighborhoods is rooted in social and economic inequities.
   (*a*) vanguard (*b*) multitude (*c*) dictum (*d*) antecedent
4. Weather predictors sometimes *foretell* weather conditions with uncanny accuracy.
   (*a*) prognosticate (*b*) verbose (*c*) traduce (*d*) impugn

5. Spring's *forerunner* in many parts of our country appearance of the crocus.
   (*a*) profusion (*b*) galaxy (*c*) precursor (*d*) apothegm
6. Citizens in the *forefront* of the conservation movement the preservation of wilderness areas.
   (*a*) vanguard (*b*) profusion (*c*) expanse (*d*) magnitude
7. Both the clinical and the cosmetic reasons for avoiding ob are *numerous.*
   (*a*) clandestine (*b*) prolix (*c*) voluble (*d*) manifold
8. The mathematics professor delivered a lecture on nucl physics which was *difficult to comprehend.*
   (*a*) recondite (*b*) commodious (*c*) legion (*d*) loquacious
9. Many political treaties are made *secretly.*
   (*a*) adage (*b*) esoteric (*c*) sub rosa (*d*) vociferous
10. *Deliberately confusing* the truth is a tactic employed in alto gether too many political situations.
    (*a*) arraying (*b*) presaging (*c*) obfuscating (*d*) glutting

obloquy defamatory language; censorious speech (*n.*)

The "soap box" orator delivered a scathing *obloquy* denouncing the perpetrators of injustice and oppression.

opprobrious infamous; scurrilous; deserving blame (*adj.*)

The *opprobrious* activities of the "robber barons" were finally curtailed by federal antitrust laws.

traduce to expose to contempt; slander (*v.t.*)

Abraham Lincoln was *traduced* in many quarters as being the perpetrator of the Civil War.

vituperate to abuse in words; censure severely (*v.t.*)

In the heat of argument many people *vituperate* their adversary, only to regret this action when tempers have had time to abate.

EXERCISES

A. Select from the following list of words those that are related to the general idea "assailing with verbal abuse."

1. vituperate
2. agglomerate
3. calumniate
4. denigrate
5. supplicate
6. obloquy
7. malign
8. piquant
9. traduce
10. opprobrious
11. salubrious
12. inveigh
13. impugn
14. egregious
15. imprecation

B. Supply the missing letters to complete a word related to the general idea "many."

1. m_ _ _ _ _
2. g_ _ _ _ _
3. l_ _ _ _ _
4. a_ _ _ _ _
5. s_ _ _ _ _
6. p_ _ _ _ _
7. m_ _ _ _ _

C. Match each word in column A with its definition in column B.

Column A	*Column B*
1. recondite	*a.* stealthy; sly
2. denigrate	*b.* that which is in the forefront
3. presage	*c.* privately; confidentially
4. legion	*d.* defamatory language
5. sub rosa	*e.* difficult to comprehend
6. obloquy	*f.* to blacken; defame
7. vanguard	*g.* a curse
8. furtive	*h.* to predict; foretell
9. inveigh (against)	*i.* a host (many)
10. imprecation	*j.* to denounce abusively

LESSON 7

In this lesson you will study words which express the *sluggish*, *superficial*, and *heedless* manner in which a thing is done. It is a casual, almost careless attitude about which we are speaking, and any of the following adjectives can be used to demonstrate this quality of inattention. If you are to benefit from this lesson, your attention to each word will have to be more than cursory.

cursory rapidly, often superficially, performed (*adj.*)

After a *cursory* examination of the file, the clerk reported the item as missing, though upon a more thorough search it was found.

desultory without order; aimless (*adj.*)

Doing a school assignment in a *desultory* fashion is courting failure.

inadvertent inattentive; heedless (*adj.*)

By an *inadvertent* remark, John disclosed the fact that a surprise party was being given for his wife.

lackadaisical listless; sluggish; dull; weak (*adj.*)

The player's *lackadaisical* manner belied his true athletic prowess.

lethargic inactive; indifferent (*adj.*)

The students' *lethargic* response to the teacher's lesson clearly indicated their complete lack of interest in the subject.

perfunctory done carelessly and superficially (*adj.*)

A *perfunctory* explanation of the issue only made things worse, since it left basic questions unanswered.

phlegmatic sluggish; apathetic (*adj.*)

Bill's *phlegmatic* attitude during the interview convinced the employer that he was too dull and lifeless for the position of radio disc jockey.

EXERCISES

A. Select from the following list of words those that are related to the general idea "sluggish, superficial, or heedless."

1. perfunctory
2. phlegmatic
3. ebullient
4. nebulous
5. desultory
6. obtuse
7. cursory
8. macabre
9. lackadaisical
10. protean
11. lethargic
12. inadvertent
13. exorbitant
14. myriad
15. empirical

B. Supply the missing letters to complete a word related to the general idea "speaking against."

1. o_ _ _ _ _
2. o_ _ _ _ _
3. i_ _ _ _ _
4. t_ _ _ _ _
5. m_ _ _ _ _
6. i_ _ _ _ _
7. c_ _ _ _ _
8. i_ _ _ _ _
9. d_ _ _ _ _
10. v_ _ _ _ _

C. Write *C* if the italicized word is consistent with the context of the sentence and *I* if it is inconsistent.

1. John was proud to declare that his friends at school were *legion.*
2. The defense attorney was pleased when the testimony of his prime witness was *impugned.*
3. His *phlegmatic* manner won the plaudits of his teacher.

4. After having scolded the student for his *opprobrious* behavior, the principal suspended him from school for three days.
5. *Maligning* your neighbors is a policy conducive to winning them as friends.
6. A doctor would conduct a thorough physical examination in a *cursory* manner.
7. A *lethargic* reaction is indicative of an indifferent attitude.
8. Any man would be proud to be *calumniated* by his friends.
9. *Vituperative* language would not ordinarily be welcomed by the person to whom it was directed.
10. A child would probably offer *sundry* reasons to his teacher for not having done his homework.

LESSON 8

If you are searching for a word to express the idea of *excess* or *needless repetition*, you have several choices. Each of the following words refers to some kind of excess. Try to determine the exact shade of meaning of each word.

cloy to fill to capacity or excess (*v.t., v.i.*)

The child's third ice cream cone temporarily *cloyed* his appetite for sweets. (*v.t.*)

Many a life story teaches that the pleasures of fame and success soon *cloy*. (*v.i.*)

inordinate excessive; unrestrained; unregulated (*adj.*)

An *inordinate* amount of starchy foods in one's diet is not conducive to the loss of weight.

jaded dulled; surfeited (*adj.*)

Many a child's appetite for learning has been *jaded* by unimaginative teaching.

plethora state of being overfull; excess (*n.*)

A *plethora* of corn resulting from a bumper harvest sent the grain market plummeting to new depths.

redundant exceeding what is usual or necessary; needlessly repetitive (*adj.*)

The *redundant* phrase "a godless atheist" was pencil-marked by the instructor.

satiate to surfeit; cloy; glut (*v.t.*)

During his vacation Oscar *satiated* himself on foreign films.

superfluous surplus; in excess of what is necessary (*adj.*)

It would be *superfluous* to report on my topic, since it was covered adequately by the main speaker.

surfeit excess; superfluity; satiety (*n.*) to cloy; overfill (*v.t.*)

An atmosphere of *surfeit* prevailed at the close of the Thanksgiving dinner. (*n.*)

One should not *surfeit* himself at the dinner table, regardless of his weight. (*v.t.*)

EXERCISES

A. Select from the following list of words those that are related to the general idea "excess, or needless repetition."

1. plethora
2. persiflage
3. proclivity
4. cloy
5. inordinate
6. redundant
7. supercilious
8. ephemeral
9. superfluous
10. hiatus
11. surfeit
12. jaded
13. anathema
14. dissipate
15. satiate

B. Supply the missing letters to complete a word related to the general idea "careless or listless."

1. d-----
2. p-----
3. l-----
4. p-----
5. c-----
6. i-----
7. l-----

C. Write *C* if the italicized word is consistent with the context of the sentence and *I* if it is inconsistent.

1. An *array* of flowers could include a wide variety of kinds.
2. You would want your character to be *denigrated* in a letter of recommendation.
3. A *phlegmatic* person is quite energetic.

4. An *obloquy* is a speech of praise.
5. A *cursory* examination is quite thorough.
6. Because the reasons for my objection are *manifold*, I cannot express them in one sentence.
7. The word scarcity is a synonym for *plethora*.
8. It is unlikely that a young man would whisper *imprecations* in his sweetheart's ear.
9. A *lethargic* person is listless and does things in a sluggish manner.
10. When a man is being *traduced*, his reputation is under attack.

LESSON 9

Have you the misfortune to number among your acquaintances or associates a person who once having made a decision will not reverse or modify it, regardless of the incontestable evidence you might offer to demonstrate the error of his thinking? He is mule-headed and *stubborn*, and will not be placated. The following words aptly characterize such a person. Make certain that you study the definitions and the illustrative sentences carefully before going on to the questions.

adamant unshakable; inflexible (*adj.*)

All offers that did not include the requested wage increase met with an *adamant* refusal.

implacable not to be appeased or pacified (*adj.*)

Most democracies are *implacable* foes of communism.

inexorable relentless; not to be persuaded by entreaty (*adj.*)

Neither promises nor threats could break the *inexorable* silence maintained by the prisoner.

intractable not capable of being easily led (*adj.*)

The *intractable* child, having exhausted his mother's patience with his incessant screaming and unruliness, finally won his own way in the matter.

obdurate stubborn; hardened in feelings (*adj.*)

Time and again the *obdurate* Pharaoh went back on his promise to Moses.

obstinate not yielding to reason or arguments (*adj.*)

The job candidate's *obstinate* requests finally won him an interview.

unyielding not submitting; not relenting (*adj.*)

His position on the matter was *unyielding*, and he would hear no more about it.

EXERCISES

A. Select from the following list of words those that are related to the general idea "stubborn or unyielding."

1. adamant
2. lascivious
3. inexorable
4. gauche
5. palpable
6. transient
7. picayune
8. obdurate
9. akimbo
10. grovel
11. intractable
12. implacable
13. adroit
14. blatant
15. obstinate

B. Supply the missing letters to complete a word related to the general idea "excess."

1. r_ _ _ _ _
2. s_ _ _ _ _
3. p_ _ _ _ _
4. s_ _ _ _ _
5. c_ _ _ _ _
6. s_ _ _ _ _
7. i_ _ _ _ _
8. j_ _ _ _ _

C. Indicate the general meaning of each of the following words by writing either "excess" or "stubborn."

1. surfeit
2. jaded
3. plethora
4. satiate
5. inexorable
6. inordinate
7. cloy
8. intractable
9. redundant
10. obdurate
11. adamant
12. superfluous
13. implacable
14. obstinate
15. unyielding

LESSON 10

Now you will study words having to do with *size*, that is, *largeness of size*. There is a host of words that aptly characterize bigness, bulkiness, or largeness. A certain amount of care must be exercised in the choice of these words, however, for some apply only to people, while others apply to things or objects. A guide to each word's usage appears in parentheses following each definition.

capacious large; roomy; spacious (things) (*adj.*)

The doctor was shown into a *capacious* room lavishly furnished in modern decor.

commodious spacious; capacious (things) (*adj.*)

The compartment on the train was surprisingly *commodious*, and we were neither crowded nor uncomfortable.

corpulent excessively fat (people) (*adj.*)

The lanky Don Quixote and his *corpulent* companion are a favorite subject of artists.

expanse wide extent (things, especially space) (*n.*)

He viewed the wide *expanse* of sky and sea with a reverent awe.

magnitudinous great in size (things) (*adj.*)

U.S. intervention in Latin American affairs has had *magnitudinous* repercussions throughout the world.

mammoth very large (people or things) (*adj.*)

A *mammoth* show was staged in the main tent of the circus.

massive large; mammoth (people or things) (*adj.*)

His *massive* frame shook violently as he argued with the pedestrian whom he had almost run down with his truck.

obese excessively fat; corpulent (people) (*adj.*)

It was difficult to determine which of the two wrestlers was the more *obese.*

voluminous of great size (things) (*adj.*)

The secretary submitted a *voluminous* report to the committee.

EXERCISES

A. Select from the following list of words those that are related to the general idea "roominess, spaciousness, or largeness of size."

1. sartorial
2. commodious
3. voluminous
4. stentorian
5. obese
6. poignant
7. gratuitous
8. massive
9. capacious
10. obsequious
11. magnitudinous
12. corpulent
13. lachrymal
14. expanse
15. mammoth

B. Supply the missing letters to complete a word related to the general idea "stubborn."

1. i-----
2. u-----
3. o-----
4. i-----
5. a-----
6. o-----
7. i-----

C. Select the word that best completes the sentence.

1. An *obese* person is (*a*) evil (*b*) fat (*c*) roomy (*d*) stubborn (*e*) talkative.
2. An *adamant* refusal is (*a*) abundant (*b*) excessive (*c*) over-filled (*d*) careless (*e*) unyielding.

3. A *redundant* expression is (*a*) going before (*b*) stubborn (*c*) superfluous (*d*) absolute (*e*) secret.
4. A *cloyed* appetite is (*a*) overfilled (*b*) cursed (*c*) large (*d*) inflexible (*e*) careless.
5. An *intractable* child is (*a*) fat (*b*) talkative (*c*) stubborn (*d*) full (*e*) hidden.
6. A *capacious* home is (*a*) sloppy (*b*) overfilled (*c*) roomy (*d*) cramped (*e*) temporary.
7. An *inordinate* amount is (*a*) exact (*b*) implied (*c*) insufficient (*d*) excessive (*e*) previous.
8. A *satiated* mind is (*a*) cursed (*b*) stubborn (*c*) voluminous (*d*) satisfied (*e*) careless.

LESSON 11

There are to be found in English—and fortunately so—many words expressing *warm praise*, *commendation*, and *approval* to balance the formidable list of negatives imputing a defamation. Should you find need of a word to express *praise* in your speaking or writing, one of the following will do very nicely.

acclamation loud, eager approval (*n.*)

A motion to adjourn the meeting for lunch was passed by unanimous *acclamation.*

adulation flattery; servile praise (*n.*)

At the height of his popularity, Elvis Presley received the *adulation* of crowds of teen-agers.

approbation act of approving (*n.*)

The committee's recommendations, when submitted to the executive board, were received with enthusiastic *approbation.*

encomium warm or high praise (*n.*)

One would not expect to hear a communist leader deliver an *encomium* on the democratic life.

eulogize to speak or write in praise of (*v.t.*)

The poet Shelley *eulogized* John Keats in his poem "Adonais."

extol to elevate by praise (*v.t.*)

Extolling the virtues of our culture to the exclusion of all others often leads to a singularity of purpose not conducive to world understanding or harmony.

laudatory expressing praise (*adj.*)

The moderator introduced the guest speaker with a few *laudatory* remarks.

panegyric eulogistic oration or writing (*n.*)

The President delivered a moving *panegyric* at the cemetery where the Medal of Honor recipient was being buried.

plaudit an applauding; figuratively, approval (*n.*)

At a special meeting in the mayor's office, the police officer received the *plaudits* of city officials for his bravery.

EXERCISES

A. Select from the following list of words those that are related to the general idea "warm praise, commendation, or approval."

1. panegyric
2. eulogize
3. plagiarize
4. bombast
5. proselyte
6. adulation
7. plaudit
8. encomium
9. delirium
10. laudatory
11. peer
12. prestidigitation
13. approbation
14. extol
15. sojourn

B. Supply the missing letters to complete a word related to the general idea "large."

1. o_ _ _ _ _
2. c_ _ _ _ _
3. c_ _ _ _ _
4. m_ _ _ _ _
5. v_ _ _ _ _
6. m_ _ _ _ _
7. m_ _ _ _ _
8. e_ _ _ _ _
9. c_ _ _ _ _

C. Write *T* if the sentence is true and *F* if it is false.

1. An *implacable* foe is unyielding.
2. *Obesity* in a person is generally undesirable.
3. A *voluminous* report is long.
4. An *adamant* position is an inflexible one.
5. A *capacious* room is not spacious.
6. To *extol* a person's virtues is to criticize them.
7. An *obdurate* view is a stubborn one.
8. To receive the *plaudits* of your employer is undesirable.
9. An *intractable* child is one whom you would enjoy having in your company.
10. A *laudatory* speech is a praising one.

D. Place beside each word the number 1 if the word refers to *largeness*, the number 2 if it refers to *stubbornness*, or the number 3 if it refers to *praise* or *commendation*. Use the following as a quick reference:

1 = large
2 = stubborn
3 = praise; commendation

1. panegyric
2. adamant
3. corpulent
4. commodious
5. adulate
6. obstinate
7. capacious
8. obese
9. extol
10. approbation
11. eulogy
12. laudatory
13. encomium
14. obdurate
15. voluminous
16. implacable
17. inexorable
18. magnitudinous
19. intractable
20. massive
21. plaudit
22. acclamation
23. unyielding

LESSON 12

In this lesson you will study words which convey the idea of *clarity*, or *that which is easily understood.* The clarity referred to concerns the understanding, as an argument or a proposition. Note the precise meaning of each of the following words; then go on to the exercises.

explicit distinctly stated; clear (*adj.*)

The captain gave *explicit* orders that no one was to leave the base.

lucid clear; pellucid; easily understood (*adj.*)

A simple but *lucid* explanation is more useful than one that is detailed but unclear.

manifest evident; obvious to the understanding; clear (*adj.*)

It was *manifest* to the instructor that one of his students had cheated on the final examination.

pellucid lucid; clear; easily understood (*adj.*)

Robert Frost's poetry is a favorite of youngsters and oldsters alike because it is *pellucid.*

perspicuous plain to the understanding; not obscure or ambiguous (*adj.*)

As a result of the lawyer's *perspicuous* argument in defense of his client, the jury found the accused not guilty of the crime.

unambiguous not obscure; clear (*adj.*)

The judge requested the attorney to rephrase his question to the witness in such a way that it would be completely *unambiguous.*

unequivocal not obscure; not ambiguous (*adj.*)

The congressman's *unequivocal* support of the bill was interpreted by his opponent as a mere attempt to gain votes.

EXERCISES

A. Select from the following list of words those that are related to the general idea "clarity or clearness, especially with regard to the understanding."

1. procrustean
2. perspicuous
3. monolithic
4. unequivocal
5. pellucid
6. esoteric
7. manifest
8. unambiguous
9. gregarious
10. sporadic
11. explicit
12. lucid
13. obtrude
14. striated
15. sophomoric

B. Supply the missing letters to complete a word related to the general idea "praise."

1. a_____
2. e_____
3. p_____
4. e_____
5. a_____
6. e_____
7. p_____
8. l_____

C. Write *S* if the words are synonyms (words having similar meanings) and *A* if they are antonyms (words having opposite meanings).

1. obese—corpulent
2. obdurate—inexorable
3. extol—defame
4. explicit—ambiguous

5. massive—minute
6. adamant—tractable
7. acclaim—laud
8. unequivocal—pellucid
9. implacable—unyielding
10. manifest—clear
11. capacious—commodious
12. perspicuous—lucid
13. panegyric—encomium
14. unambiguous—unequivocal
15. intractable—unyielding

D. Select the word that is most closely related in meaning to the given word.

1. loquacious: (*a*) secret (*b*) talkative (*c*) stubborn
2. dictum: (*a*) listless (*b*) adage (*c*) praise
3. recondite: (*a*) profound (*b*) precursor (*c*) massive
4. harbinger: (*a*) vanguard (*b*) curse (*c*) saying
5. plethora: (*a*) excess (*b*) obdurate (*c*) clarity
6. malign: (*a*) secret (*b*) praise (*c*) slander
7. lethargic: (*a*) phlegmatic (*b*) obdurate (*c*) unclear
8. superfluous: (*a*) unyielding (*b*) maxim (*c*) excess
9. obdurate: (*a*) esoteric (*b*) inflexible (*c*) tractable
10. obese: (*a*) fat (*b*) praise (*c*) secret
11. encomium: (*a*) praise (*b*) surfeit (*c*) curse
12. verbose: (*a*) malign (*b*) manifest (*c*) wordy
13. maxim: (*a*) much (*b*) adage (*c*) prolix
14. esoteric: (*a*) secret (*b*) garrulous (*c*) clear
15. precursor: (*a*) plethora (*b*) vanguard (*c*) lucidity
16. surfeit: (*a*) cloy (*b*) calumniate (*c*) praise
17. obloquy: (*a*) augur (*b*) slander (*c*) encomium

18. phlegmatic: (*a*) prognosticate (*b*) sluggish (*c*) secret

19. redundant: (*a*) superfluous (*b*) obdurate (*c*) roomy

20. implacable: (*a*) cursory (*b*) tractable (*c*) unyielding

21. corpulent: (*a*) obese (*b*) satiate (*c*) listless

22. eulogy: (*a*) obloquy (*b*) massive (*c*) praise

23. imprecation: (*a*) curse (*b*) redundant (*c*) precursor

24. cloyed: (*a*) satiated (*b*) inadvertent (*c*) adamant

25. sub rosa: (*a*) secretly (*b*) eulogy (*c*) slander

LESSON 13

Now assume that you wish to convey to your reader or listener the idea of *brevity* or the *fleeting quality of time.* The moment is here, and then in a flickering of a second it is gone. You may use any of the following words, and your idea will be stated both succinctly and unambiguously.

ephemeral short-lived; having a brief life or influence (*adj.*)

Viewed from the aspect of eternity, a man's life span is manifestly *ephemeral.*

evanescent fleeting; momentary (*adj.*)

Many groups that play popular music have brilliant but *evanescent* careers.

fugitive passing quickly; liable to fade (*adj.*)

The *fugitive* years of youth seem to escape us before we are able to use them wisely.

temporal pertaining to time; worldly (as opposed to *eternal, immortal*) (*adj.*)

Pain and pleasure are integral facets of man's *temporal* existence.

transient short-lived (*adj.*)

The *transient* quality of fame is poignantly captured in Housman's poem "To An Athlete Dying Young."

transitory not enduring; bound to pass (*adj.*)

A *transitory* feeling of excitement pervaded the room as the president announced the promotion list.

EXERCISES

A. Select from the following list of words those that are related to the general idea "fleeting, short-lived, or brief."

1. tawdry
2. transient
3. venial
4. halcyon
5. fugitive
6. quixotic
7. evanescent
8. ecumenical
9. ephemeral
10. maudlin
11. sycophant
12. temporal
13. onerous
14. heinous
15. transitory

B. Supply the missing letters to complete a word related to the general idea "clear."

1. p- - - - -
2. p- - - - -
3. u- - - - -
4. u- - - - -
5. m- - - - -
6. e- - - - -
7. l- - - - -

C. Select the word that is closest in meaning to the italicized word or phrase.

1. Most vacation romances are *short-lived*, since they last only as long as the vacation.
   (*a*) profuse (*b*) esoteric (*c*) transitory (*d*) obdurate
2. *Defaming or blackening* a man's good name is a tactic not uncommon to American politics.
   (*a*) surfeiting (*b*) denigrating (*c*) glutting (*d*) auguring
3. The doctor told his patient that the postoperative symptoms were *not permanent* and would soon disappear.
   (*a*) profuse (*b*) transient (*c*) implacable (*d*) esoteric
4. The popular *saying* "Nothing succeeds like success" though trite is nonetheless true.
   (*a*) eulogy (*b*) encomium (*c*) adage (*d*) harbinger

5. One's taste for television can soon be *overfilled* by the pabulum-type fare provided the viewer.
   (*a*) cloyed (*b*) impugned (*c*) denigrated (*d*) traduced
6. Doing your work in a *careless or heedless* manner does not invite success.
   (*a*) jaded (*b*) prolix (*c*) furtive (*d*) perfunctory
7. The *abstruse* language of some sciences proves to be a hindrance to many students.
   (*a*) jaded (*b*) esoteric (*c*) effete (*d*) obdurate
8. The senator was a *vocally loud* opponent of the proposed bill.
   (*a*) vociferous (*b*) esoteric (*c*) recondite (*d*) covert
9. The *secret* meeting of the enemy agents was made known.
   (*a*) garrulous (*b*) loquacious (*c*) vociferous (*d*) clandestine
10. Most instructors in English complain that student writing is *wordy*.
    (*a*) surreptitious (*b*) prolix (*c*) jaded (*d*) esoteric

LESSON 14

The following words have as a common denominator that which is *harmful*, *antagonistic*, or *not beneficial*. The harm implicit in these words can affect a person's physical or mental well-being.

baneful poisonous; pernicious (*adj.*)

The *baneful* effects of uninformed criticism often outreach the supposed ills toward which it is directed.

deleterious hurtful; noxious (*adj.*)

Many doctors believe that smoking has a *deleterious* effect on one's health.

inimical unfriendly; antagonistic (*adj.*)

Communist doctrine in action is *inimical* to the best interests of the democratic political philosophy.

insalubrious not beneficial or helpful (*adj.*)

The speaker's apparent stage fright had an *insalubrious* effect on his delivery.

noxious harmful; unwholesome (*adj.*)

Carbon monoxide fumes are *noxious.*

pernicious intending evil; wicked (*adj.*)

Cancer is a *pernicious* disease.

unpropitious not helpful; not favorable (*adj.*)

The *unpropitious* predictions about the weather forced the officers to postpone the Student Government outing.

EXERCISES

A. Select from the following list of words those that are related to the general idea "harmful, antagonistic, or not beneficial."

1. inimical
2. noxious
3. sardonic
4. travesty
5. pernicious
6. acumen
7. unpropitious
8. pneumatic
9. baneful
10. insalubrious
11. ostracize
12. vixen
13. mercenary
14. deleterious
15. obese

B. Supply the missing letters to complete a word related to the general idea "passing or temporary."

1. t-----
2. e-----
3. e-----
4. t-----
5. f-----
6. t-----

C. Write *T* if the sentence is true and *F* if it is false.

1. A *transient* experience is extended over a long period of time.
2. That which is *deleterious* is beneficial.
3. You would hope for an *unpropitious* event to occur in your life.
4. One's lifetime is *ephemeral* when viewed from the aspect of eternity.
5. You would attempt to subvert that which was *inimical* to your best interests.

LESSON 15

The following words are very closely related in that they all denote *greediness.* The literal connotation of these words is negative, but sometimes the words can be used in a context that indicates a positive quality. For example, one who eats voraciously is—and with good reason—criticized for his piggish table manners; however, were this same person a voracious reader, it would be another matter. You could not justifiably condemn a person who has an insatiable appetite for reading. Hence the sentence in which you find the word will determine whether or not the word is used in an unfavorable sense.

avaricious having an inordinate desire for wealth; implies both miserliness and greed (*adj.*)

The *avaricious* Judas betrayed Christ for thirty pieces of silver.

covet to desire; long for something that belongs to another (*v.t.*)

It is morally wrong to *covet* your neighbor's material goods.

cupidity greed; inordinate desire for wealth (*n.*)

Man's *cupidity*, not God's will, is responsible for many of the injustices existing on earth.

glut to swallow, especially, greedily (*v.t.*)

Having *glutted* itself on its prey, the lion disappeared into the jungle.

rapacious grasping or covetous (*adj.*)

Attila the Hun, a *rapacious* leader of barbarians, plundered and devastated the ancient city of Rome.

ravenous greedy; marked by excessive hunger (*adj.*)

After having trekked through the woods all day, the hunters returned to camp, bringing with them *ravenous* appetites.

voracious greedy in eating (*adj.*)

His appetite for reading Shakespeare was *voracious.*

EXERCISES

A. Select from the following list of words those that are related to the general idea "greed."

1. avaricious
2. sarcophagus
3. iconoclast
4. amortize
5. covet
6. rapacious
7. harridan
8. cupidity
9. ravenous
10. bane
11. mollify
12. glut
13. genuflect
14. abyss
15. voracious

B. Supply the missing letters to complete a word related to the general idea "harmful."

1. u-----
2. i-----
3. p-----
4. n-----
5. d-----
6. b-----
7. i-----

C. Select the word that is most closely related in meaning to the given word.

1. harbinger: (*a*) vanguard (*b*) robin (*c*) secret
2. plethora: (*a*) augur (*b*) saying (*c*) excess
3. maxim: (*a*) proverb (*b*) praise (*c*) prelude

4. vociferous: (*a*) loud (*b*) careless (*c*) secret
5. surreptitious: (*a*) overt (*b*) clandestine (*c*) obstinate
6. phlegmatic: (*a*) listless (*b*) numerous (*c*) obese
7. adamant: (*a*) obdurate (*b*) denigrate (*c*) massive
8. obese: (*a*) corpulent (*b*) perspicuous (*c*) satiate
9. perfunctory: (*a*) careless (*b*) commodious (*c*) surreptitious
10. rapacious: (*a*) redundant (*b*) voracious (*c*) covert
11. encomium: (*a*) apothegm (*b*) curse (*c*) eulogy
12. unambiguous: (*a*) lucid (*b*) perfunctory (*c*) ephemeral
13. cloy: (*a*) overfill (*b*) obese (*c*) vituperate
14. baneful: (*a*) listless (*b*) harmful (*c*) obstinate
15. ravenous: (*a*) transitory (*b*) commodious (*c*) rapacious

LESSON 16

This next list of words has to do with *vocal punishment*, or *scolding*. There may be a difference in the degree of punishing implicit in these words, but basically there is not so great a disparity as to preclude their being presented in one lesson. Make certain that you understand the meaning and the proper context of each word before moving on to the exercises.

admonish to warn gently but seriously (*v.t.*)

The principal *admonished* the student who, while running down the corridor, knocked a young girl to the ground.

castigate to administer severe verbal punishment (*v.t.*)

The judge *castigated* the accused before passing sentence.

censure to criticize with authority (*v.t.*)

Because he was publicly *censured*, the instructor submitted his resignation to the college's president.

chide to utter words of reproof; scold (*v.t.*)

There are those psychologists who believe that to *chide* a youngster occasionally has a salubrious effect on both child and parent.

rebuke to give sharp reproof or stern criticism (*v.t.*)

The judge *rebuked* the witness for not answering the questions.

reprimand to scold formally or officially (*v.t.*)

The policeman *reprimanded* the driver for having passed a stop sign in a school zone.

reproach to blame; express dissatisfaction with (*v.t.*)

Lewis *reproached* his parents, telling them that they did not understand his generation.

reprove to blame, usually in a well-meaning way (*v.t.*)

To *reprove* a child too often is as harmful as no reproofs at all.

upbraid to scold in righteous anger (*v.t.*)

While John was being *upbraided* by his teacher, young Mary was snickering and thoroughly enjoying the situation.

EXERCISES

A. Select from the following list of words those that are related to the general idea "punishing or scolding."

1. prevaricate
2. castigate
3. admonish
4. scintillate
5. reprove
6. chide
7. suborn
8. reprimand
9. upbraid
10. bellicose
11. reproach
12. iniquity
13. censure
14. rebuke
15. stigma

B. Supply the missing letters to complete a word related to the general idea "greed or extreme hunger."

1. r-----
2. a-----
3. c-----
4. g-----
5. r-----
6. v-----
7. c-----

C. Write *C* if the italicized word is consistent with the context of the sentence and *I* if it is inconsistent.

1. Under normal circumstances you would enjoy being *chided.*
2. All doctors agree that the use of narcotics does not have a *pernicious* effect on the user.

3. *Ravenous* eating habits are highly desirable and should be practiced.
4. If you violated the law and were apprehended, you could reasonably expect to be *censured.*
5. *Glutting* oneself at the dinner table is not only impolite but also unhealthful.
6. Were a doctor to inform you that smoking cigarettes was having a *deleterious* effect on your health, you should give them up.
7. You would probably not wish to have as your neighbor a person who is *covetous.*
8. A *noxious* substance is harmful.
9. After having *admonished* the jaywalker, the policeman let her off with a stern warning.
10. An *ephemeral* quality is an enduring one.

D. Select the word that is most closely related in meaning to the given word.

1. verbose: (*a*) wordy (*b*) pithy (*c*) cursed
2. sundry: (*a*) legion (*b*) esoteric (*c*) harmful
3. apothegm: (*a*) adage (*b*) excess (*c*) array
4. augur: (*a*) anodyne (*b*) curse (*c*) predict
5. garrulous: (*a*) array (*b*) loquacious (*c*) hidden
6. prelude: (*a*) prefatory event (*b*) exoteric (*c*) praise
7. prolix: (*a*) sundry (*b*) wordy (*c*) large
8. array: (*a*) augur (*b*) sundry (*c*) adulate
9. esoteric: (*a*) secret (*b*) prolix (*c*) excess
10. aphorism: (*a*) adage (*b*) garrulous (*c*) secret
11. furtive: (*a*) sly (*b*) lucid (*c*) inadvertent
12. traduce: (*a*) defame (*b*) eulogize (*c*) predict
13. obloquy: (*a*) encomium (*b*) defamatory speech (*c*) truism
14. denigrate: (*a*) defame (*b*) cursory (*c*) precede
15. obdurate: (*a*) cursory (*b*) corpulent (*c*) adamant

16. cursory: (*a*) perfunctory (*b*) lucid (*c*) recondite

17. vituperate: (*a*) traduce (*b*) cloy (*c*) foresee

18. redundant: (*a*) repetitious (*b*) pellucid (*c*) clandestine

19. malign: (*a*) defame (*b*) eulogize (*c*) augur

20. perspicuous: (*a*) lucid (*b*) redundant (*c*) esoteric

LESSON 17

The following words are definitely not synonyms. They are, however, related in that they all imply *oldness* or *old age*. Some of these words are more applicable to people, while others are more applicable to things. Some, like *effete* and *venerable*, can apply to either people or things. The illustrative sentences show an appropriate use of each word.

antiquated grown old; out of style (*adj.*)

The *antiquated* farmhouse was converted into a restaurant and flourished in its rustic setting.

archaic of an earlier, more primitive time (*adj.*)

Should you look in a dictionary and find "*archaic*" listed beside the meaning of a word, it indicates that this particular word is no longer in current use.

dotage feeblemindedness, especially in senility (*n.*)

Senility and *dotage* cause many of our senior citizens to be institutionalized for their own safety.

effete worn out with age (*adj.*)

The Roman Empire was already an *effete* civilization by the time the first kingdoms appeared in Europe.

senile characteristic of old age (*adj.*)

When a person becomes *senile* we say that he is entering second childhood.

superannuated no longer active or useful because of age (*adj.*)

The horse-drawn buggy has in our modern age become a *superannuated* relic of the past.

venerable worthy of worship; generally implies advanced age (*adj.*)

The *venerable* tradition of Thanksgiving has been handed down to us for generations.

EXERCISES

A. Select from the following list of words those that are related to the general idea "old or out of date."

1. senile
2. superfluous
3. superannuated
4. solecism
5. dotage
6. stalemate
7. benedict
8. curate
9. venerable
10. effete
11. venal
12. platitude
13. antiquated
14. archaic
15. acolyte

B. Supply the missing letters to complete a word related to the general idea "blame."

1. c-----
2. r-----
3. a-----
4. c-----
5. c-----
6. r-----
7. r-----
8. r-----
9. u-----

C. Select the word that is closest in meaning to the italicized word or phrase.

1. On the basis of a *superficial* examination, the doctor made a diagnosis which later proved to be incorrect.
(*a*) cursory (*b*) adamant (*c*) rapacious (*d*) lucid
2. The mentally deranged patient had moments of *clear* thinking before lapsing again into his world of fantasy.
(*a*) obdurate (*b*) lucid (*c*) redundant (*d*) adamant

3. A *dull, listless* demeanor certainly would not impress your prospective employer.
   (*a*) lucid (*b*) perspicuous (*c*) phlegmatic (*d*) commodious
4. The hotel guest was ushered into a *large, spacious* room overlooking the lake nestled among the mountains.
   (*a*) commodious (*b*) redundant (*c*) obdurate (*d*) phlegmatic
5. The *fat* gentleman mopped his brow with a large red handkerchief.
   (*a*) rapacious (*b*) adamant (*c*) prolix (*d*) corpulent
6. A partial loss of vision and hearing are ills usually attending *old age.*
   (*a*) obloquy (*b*) senility (*c*) lethargy (*d*) verbosity
7. In his declining years, the *worn out with age* ruler left the management of the kingdom to his ministers.
   (*a*) clandestine (*b*) commodious (*c*) effete (*d*) lucid
8. Many people will store away in an attic items which have become *old.*
   (*a*) antiquated (*b*) garrulous (*c*) commodious (*d*) unambiguous
9. Dictionaries list words no longer in current use as being *out of date.*
   (*a*) perfunctory (*b*) unambiguous (*c*) archaic (*d*) lucid
10. The *plundering* Vandals who sacked Rome destroyed many irreplaceable works of art.
    (*a*) lethargic (*b*) verbose (*c*) rapacious (*d*) effete

LESSON 18

Once again, the words in this lesson are not synonyms. They do, however, enjoy a common denominator which makes it possible to study them in one lesson. This kinship which exists among them relates to the idea of *weakness or ineffectualness.*

debilitate to impair the strength of; weaken (*v.t.*)

Smoking *debilitates* those who participate in track and field sporting events.

enervate to deprive of force or strength (*v.t.*)

The oppressive climate of the tropics *enervates* those who are not accustomed to it.

impotent lacking power or strength (*adj.*)

The judge charged that justice was being perverted since the court was rendered *impotent* as a result of the jury's decision.

infirm not sound physically; weak, especially from age (*adj.*)

A man may be *infirm* in body and yet be as acute as ever in his mind.

languish to lose strength or vitality because of outward circumstances; lose force (*v.i.*)

In many Elizabethan sonnets the lover *languishes* in despair over his unrequited love.

moribund in a dying state (*adj.*)

Communists maintain that the American democratic way is *moribund.*

nugatory of no force; ineffectual (*adj.*)

The *nugatory* Nationalist Chinese Government set up its headquarters on the island of Formosa.

EXERCISES

A. Select from the following list of words those that are related to the general idea "weakness or ineffectualness."

1. nugatory
2. bucolic
3. nepotism
4. adumbrate
5. languish
6. enervate
7. procrastinate
8. debilitate
9. impugn
10. infirm
11. deride
12. coquette
13. subsidiary
14. moribund
15. impotent

B. Supply the missing letters to complete a word related to the general idea "old."

1. a- - - - -
2. s- - - - -
3. s- - - - -
4. d- - - - -
5. v- - - - -
6. a- - - - -
7. e- - - - -

C. Write *C* if the italicized word is consistent with the context of the sentence and *I* if it is inconsistent.

1. An *archaic* expression is one which is outdated.
2. A *nugatory* law is one which is enforced to the letter.
3. Many civilizations which at one time were world powers are now *effete*.
4. Boarded-up store fronts testified to the *moribund* state of local business.
5. A *superannuated* custom would be practiced regularly.

D. Select the word that is most closely related in meaning to the given word.

1. loquacious: (*a*) talkative (*b*) secret (*c*) abundant
2. legion: (*a*) secret (*b*) many (*c*) careless
3. adage: (*a*) maxim (*b*) plethora (*c*) praise
4. clandestine: (*a*) secret (*b*) verbose (*c*) excess
5. prognosticate: (*a*) predict (*b*) voluble (*c*) fleeting
6. anodyne: (*a*) furtive (*b*) adage (*c*) prolix
7. sub rosa: (*a*) capacious (*b*) secretly (*c*) clear
8. galaxy: (*a*) cloy (*b*) parables (*c*) many
9. corpulent: (*a*) obese (*b*) obdurate (*c*) transient
10. eulogize: (*a*) denigrate (*b*) scold (*c*) praise
11. satiate: (*a*) overfill (*b*) eulogize (*c*) harm
12. commodious: (*a*) roomy (*b*) lucid (*c*) superfluous
13. unyielding: (*a*) intractable (*b*) perspicuous (*c*) lackadaisical
14. lucid: (*a*) cloy (*b*) large (*c*) clear
15. ephemeral: (*a*) baneful (*b*) laudatory (*c*) fleeting

LESSON 19

The following list of words has in common a *premeditated counterfeiting* or *deceitful behavior*. The deceit may be in the form of a blatant lie or an underhanded trick or ruse. Remember, these words are not synonyms but, rather, are related in a general way as to the ideas they convey.

chicanery deception; trickery, especially in legal proceedings (*n.*)

Many unscrupulous lawyers, though knowing their clients to be guilty, defend and absolve them from blame through some form of *chicanery*.

dissemble to hide under a false semblance; feign (*v.t.*, *v.i.*)

The person who *dissembles* his errors may find it an expensive and time-consuming undertaking. (*v.t.*)
It was plain to everyone that the witness was *dissembling* out of fear of reprisal. (*v.i.*)

guile deceitful cunning; craft and trickery (*n.*)

Feminine *guile* has brought about the downfall of many men through the years, Samson being the most famous and unfortunate example.

malinger to feign illness in order to avoid doing one's duty (*v.i.*)

Many men who were drafted into the armed forces *malingered* constantly in the hope of being medically discharged.

mendacious given to falsehood; lying (*adj.*)

Mendacious persons are usually found out to be what they are and as a consequence are not trusted by their associates.

prevaricate to lie, especially by speaking ambiguously or evasively (*v.i.*)

When a person *prevaricates* we are not sure whether he is saying "yes" or "no."

specious apparently fair, just, or correct but in fact not so; false (*adj.*)

The audience was duped by the speaker whose *specious* argument convinced them that his cause was just.

spurious not genuine; false; counterfeit (*adj.*)

The counterfeiter was apprehended by the police as he attempted to foist on the storekeeper a *spurious* ten dollar bill.

EXERCISES

A. Select from the following list of words those that are related to the general idea "falseness or premeditated counterfeiting; deceitful behavior."

1. supplant
2. dissemble
3. affront
4. malinger
5. prevaricate
6. propitiate
7. vacillate
8. specious
9. exhume
10. satiate
11. chicanery
12. jargon
13. spurious
14. guile
15. mendacious

B. Supply the missing letters to complete a word related to the general idea "weak."

1. n_ _ _ _ _
2. i_ _ _ _ _
3. e_ _ _ _ _
4. d_ _ _ _ _
5. m_ _ _ _ _
6. l_ _ _ _ _
7. i_ _ _ _ _

C. Write *S* if the words are synonyms and *A* if they are antonyms.

1. dissembling—feigning
2. prevaricate—lie
3. archaic—modern
4. nugatory—effectual
5. specious—false
6. chicanery—deception
7. superannuated—antiquated
8. infirm—strong
9. guile—treachery
10. mendacious—honest
11. enervated—debilitated
12. feign—prevaricate
13. languish—strengthen
14. spurious—counterfeit
15. moribund—flourishing

LESSON 20

For our final formal lesson, you will deal with a group of words which mean *to appeal to*, *to beg*, or *to plead*. Some of these words are almost identical in meaning, but you will see from the illustrative sentences that they all have slightly different applications.

adjure to appeal to solemnly (*v.t.*)

Initiates into the secret society were *adjured* never to reveal its membership or its codes.

beseech to beg urgently; supplicate (*v.t.*)

The distraught mother cried, "I *beseech* you; please do not allow this terrible thing to happen to my son!"

entreat to beg; attempt to persuade (*v.t.*, *v.i.*)

In his final speech the defense attorney *entreated* the jury to consider his defendant's misfortunes before offering their verdict. (*v.t.*)
After the child had *entreated* for an hour, her mother relented and allowed her to watch television. (*v.i.*)

implore to make an urgent plea; beg (*v.t.*)

The hostage *implored* his captor to set him free.

importune to plead persistently (*v.t.*, *v.i.*)

Lionel *importuned* his brother to let him get up off the ground. (*v.t.*)
The woman who was late for the bus *importuned* with the attendant, but to no avail. (*v.i.*)

invoke to appeal to for support (*v.t.*)

The high priest *invoked* the spirit of the ancestor who had been offended.

supplicate to make a humble request; ask earnestly or prayerfully of (*v.t., v.i.*)

The convict's mother *supplicated* the governor to commute the death sentence imposed on her son. (*v.t.*)
During periods of drought the high priest would *supplicate* for rain. (*v.i.*)

EXERCISES

A. Select from the following list of words those that are related to the general idea "appealing to or begging."

1. supplicate
2. manifest
3. trepidation
4. expedite
5. importune
6. adjure
7. imprecate
8. sanctimony
9. beseech
10. analogy
11. entreat
12. emancipate
13. shibboleth
14. invoke
15. implore

B. Supply the missing letters to complete a word related to the general idea "false."

1. m_ _ _ _ _
2. g_ _ _ _ _
3. p_ _ _ _ _
4. d_ _ _ _ _
5. m_ _ _ _ _
6. s_ _ _ _ _
7. c_ _ _ _ _
8. s_ _ _ _ _

C. Write *C* if the italicized word is consistent with the context of the sentence and *I* if it is inconsistent.

1. A *spurious* painting is authentic.
2. A *nugatory* government is effectual.
3. *Malingering* will get you far in your work.
4. A *dissembler* is one who pretends.
5. Prayers to God might include *supplications.*
6. An honest person would seek out someone *mendacious* for a friend.
7. His *moribund* schedule kept him constantly on the go.
8. A sprightly person is usually one who is *enervated.*
9. The convict *languished* in prison for ten years before he died.
10. It would be advisable for an attorney to practice *chicanery* in his lawsuits.

D. Write *S* if the words are synonyms, *A* if they are antonyms, or *N* if they are neither synonyms nor antonyms.

1. superannuated—contemporary
2. guile—treachery
3. entreat—feign
4. beseech—supplicate
5. debilitate—enervate
6. infirm—importune
7. adjure—entreat
8. dotage—feeblemindedness
9. moribund—dying
10. supplicate—entreat